IS GOD
STILL IN THE
HEALING
BUSINESS?

IS GOD
STILL IN THE
HEALING
BUSINESS?

DAVID MARSHALL

AUTUMN

HOUSE

ISBN 1-873796-36-6

Published by
Autumn House Limited
Alma Park, Grantham, Lincs., NG31 9SL, England

About the author

Dr. David Marshall has pastoral, teaching and journalistic experience. He has a first degree and a PhD from the University of Hull. From 1979 to 1993 he edited *Family Life* magazine. At present he is almost certainly the most prolific Christian author in Britain.

Dr. Marshall is married, lives in Lincolnshire, and is part of a large, three-tiered family.

Other books by David Marshall

WHERE JESUS WALKED (1986)

BREADFRUIT, BUCCANEERS AND THE BOUNTY BIBLE (1987)

THE BATTLE FOR THE BOOK (1991)

THE DEVIL HIDES OUT (1991)

NEW AGE VERSUS THE GOSPEL (1993)

PILGRIM WAYS (1993)

All published by Autumn House.

AN INTRODUCTION TO THE LIFE AND WORKS OF JOHN BUNYAN (1989)

Published by Bishopsgate.

Thanks

to Jennifer Rees Larcombe for submitting to our
interminable questions, answering them so patiently and
comprehensively and, in so doing, providing the seed-corn
ideas for this book;
to my colleague Barry Alen, who not only designed the cover
but inspired chapter 8 *and* introduced me to the work of
American author Philip Yancey who has given more thought
to the 'Why is God Silent?' question than anyone else I
know.

Contents

If you could ask God one question, what would it be?

That was the question that National Opinion Poll put to a 'representative sample' of 1,894 people on behalf of a Sunday newspaper.

They published the findings, jokers and all:

Why wasn't I born rich?

Can I have a Porsche Turbo?

May I marry Arnold Schwartzenegger?

Why do you tolerate the present government?

But those were the maverick questions. Not typical.

The typical questions included two elements: real concern about the problems of the world; anger and frustration with God for allowing them or not tackling them. One man screamed, 'WHY? WHY? WHY? GOD!'

Most were more specific. 'God, if You've got all that power, why do millions starve in the Third World? Why are there so many wars? Why do You let the innocent suffer?'

The Christian segment of the sample homed in closer:

Why do bad things happen to good people?

Why do You heal some people and not others?

Why are You silent? Have You given up on the direct intervention option?

Why did my wife die of cancer?

Is suffering supposed to help us?

God, are you still in the healing business?

Here we have had a stab at answering those questions.

The questions have been examined against a background of certain authenticated cases in which God *has* healed, and equally well-documented cases in which He has *not* healed.

The questions have also been examined against a background of the available biblical data.

But, be warned. God has never written a fully comprehensive essay answering the 'Why suffering?' question. We have clues, pointers and a framework for faith. We do not pretend to have all the answers. We invite you to suspect anyone who claims he does . . . .

DAVID MARSHALL

1 Out of a clear blue sky

'It exploded like a bomb. There was this terrible pain in my head and neck. It wouldn't go away. I began to see double. I couldn't grip things . . . .'

This is how Jennifer Rees Larcombe describes the onset of *viral encephalitis*, an illness that involves a chronic inflammation of the muscles; and attacks the meninges, the nerve-casings and the brain.

The explosion in Jen's body came without warning. The pain was horrendous. A friend phoned the doctor. She was in hospital within the hour.

Soon she was part of a surreal world, flat on her back, hurtling at speed through hospital corridors with nothing to see but the ceiling lights. Bright lights *and faces*. Confusing faces. Faces with mouths where their eyes should be.

Life had gone seriously wrong. What was happening to Tony and their six children? Pain, throbbing, pulsating, convulsed her whole body. Why couldn't she move her limbs? Why had they put the cot sides up? 'Is *this* what it feels like to go mad?'

Jen tried to cry out, but could produce no sound. There were faces again. Tony's face? She wanted to say to him: 'Marry again if I die.'

Fear, sour like brass in the mouth . . . and Death hovering on the margins of her vision. But she was a Christian and unafraid of death . . . .

Amid the loneliness, she knew she feared Death above all.

Then Death moved in from the margins . . . breathing and swallowing were impossibilities, and somebody seemed to have taken her heart in a tight fist — and was twisting and wrenching it. Death at that moment seemed friendly. An end of pain.

But what was happening? The bed was surrounded by figures. Urgent voices. Strong hands doing painful things to her. Resuscitation. And the return of pain. Jen did not know it, but she had been moved to a specialist hospital in London. Little by little it dawned on her consciousness that her body had ceased to function. It was no longer under her control.

Home was out of the question.

In time, Jen was moved to Burrswood, a Christian convalescent centre in idyllic surroundings, where prayer was considered as potent as medicine.[1] She remembers someone pushing her in a wheelchair into the chapel. Worried about Tony, frantic about the children, Jen tried to verbalize a prayer for healing.

Noise jangled her nerves. When she touched things she felt harsh pain. How could she ever go home to the rough-and-scramble of family life?

Duncan, her 6-year-old son, minus his mother, was having problems at school. Somehow aware of that, Jen tried to reach out to him, to lay her hand on his shoulder when Tony brought him to visit. But her arms and legs would not do what she wanted them to do. She managed no more than an ugly twitch. She tried to make words. They would not come. Then when they did they were slurred, drunken. Revulsion registered on Duncan's features. Jen saw him run into a corner and heard him scream uncontrollably.

Some slight improvement — and Tony's persuasion — brought Jen home only four weeks later. It was a disaster from the start. She couldn't grip, or walk. Her bowels and bladder were out of control. Humiliation. Frustration. What use was she to her family?

And there was no escaping the pain: at the base of the skull, down the spine, sometimes everywhere at once.

Things were not going well for Tony. He wanted to walk away. His wife and the mother of his children — in a nappy? But the solemn vows of marriage were binding. He resolved to carry on and face whatever future there was.

Jen had to watch what was happening to her formerly well-behaved, full-of-life children. Nervousness and long faces. Bed-wetting, school phobia and truancy, aggression: life was falling apart.

The medicine men looked grave, and said profound things. At least the neurologist was frank. She would never get any better than she was then. She had to accept the state of things and learn to live within her limits.

Disaster had struck out of a clear blue sky and rendered her a no-hoper.

---

[1] Burrswood, associated with the name of Dorothy Kerin, is the most outstanding example of a number of 'homes of healing' set up in England. See Rex Gardner, *A Doctor Investigates Healing Miracles* (Darton, Longman and Todd, 1986) page 57 *et seq*.

2 Face down in the mud

As time passed, Jen's mind demisted She could speak again. She saw clearly the awful picture that was life. The doctors had given up on her. She had to look for another way.

As a Christian, Jen knew about divine healing. She asked lots of questions, listened to endless cassettes, was the centre of stage-managed healing-services at Christian centres. With every failure came Job's comforters, each with his own theory as to why she was not getting better. And, Jen discovered, the arguments had not progressed since Job. The favourite? There was some unconfessed secret sin in her life.

'Do you have to be perfect to be healed?' Jen pondered. 'Were those whom Jesus healed perfect people? The ten lepers? The two demoniacs . . . ?' She had accepted Jesus' death on the cross for her sins. She was saved by His life, His death, His holiness. Wasn't that it?

Then there were those who said she simply didn't have enough faith . . . .

Jen hit the pits. It was the day before the family moved from their home in the country to a house in the town, a move necessitated by Jen's condition. Just one more time she wanted to get out in the green fields where she, Tony and the family had run and played so happily together. She *did* have those two sticks. If she could only make it to the gap in the hedge at the end of the garden . . . .

It took hours of wobble, lurch and struggle; but she made it. Beyond the gap in the hedge, rolling green fields. All she had to do was to walk the plank across a quagmire of mud churned up by the cows. Her balance gave. Before she knew it, she was face down in the mud, and manure . . . .

In the hours it took Tony to find her, Jen had plenty of time to think. 'Here's what it's come to. My life's just a sea of muck. And the more I struggle, the deeper I shall be mired in it.'

Looking back, Jen feels that *that* was the most important point in her experience. No divine voice spoke through thunder or earthquake. She cannot categorically state that a still small voice whispered in her ear. Jen just *knew*. God had spoken. In the midst of the mess, *He* was with her.

In the hours Jen and God spent face down in the mud, she gave Him the broken pieces of her life, her body, her marriage and her family. She gave Him, too, all her hurt and her anguish. In exchange, He gave her a new mind-set: in one sense a new life.

Once Jen was indoors and washed down, and after a good laugh, Tony and the children saw that Mum was different. In the ensuing days, the children invented a word for God's gift to Mum: *peace-joy*.

It was in 1984 when the Larcombes moved from the country to the house in Tunbridge Wells. Jen received both mobility and severe disability allowances from the DHSS — at the highest possible rate; and, at the cost of thousands, a lift, ramps and rails for her wheelchair were installed in the new home.

The children took to taking Mum for rides in her wheelchair. At Duncan's sports day she entered the mothers' race, he pushing her! At home she began to write again. She had published a number of children's books before her illness. With help, and over long weeks, she learned to stab her index finger into a keyboard Tony had bought. When the manuscript was completed, Jen found a publisher. *Beyond Healing* (Hodder) was a best-seller in Christian bookshops. Then she was in demand as a public speaker.

But there were down times. Especially on holiday. Jen in her wheelchair, Tony and the six children just dots on distant cliffs. They travelled up to London for the day, Jen and her wheelchair among the freight in the guard's van.

When Tony secured a taxi at Waterloo, one Young, Upwardly Mobile Person pushed in front. 'Hold up, moyte,' said the cabby, 'Can't ya see, I've got a bleedin' cripple 'ere!'

Jen had promised God to stop pestering Him about healing. He had to take the initiative. Right?

Year after year the DHSS gave Jen maximum disability allowance, without requiring further assessments.

But, from March 1990, in her moments of peace-joy, it seemed to Jen that God was telling her He wanted to heal her. Having been told, repeatedly, that she could expect no improvement, Jen told herself that her imagination was in overdrive. Perhaps it was the last vestige of wishful thinking from her subconscious. She had been completely disabled for eight years. 'No more healing services,' thought Jen; if it *was* God who was speaking He would send someone to pray for her.

Over the next three months, every time the doorbell rang Jen wondered if God had sent somebody. Again she tried to will herself better, but her efforts left her face down in the mud — metaphorically, this time.

Meanwhile, the pain seemed to get worse, and the humiliation of her failure to control her body increased. Despite all, she kept up her speaking engagements.

One day, at the Three Counties Church, Hazelmere, her pain was so intense that her talk was, at best, mechanical. In the question-and-answer session the pain prevented Jen from hearing clearly. So the first time Wendy Cashmore said what she said, Jen had to ask her to repeat it. Wendy was, in any event, very hesitant and appeared covered with confusion:

'I'm very sorry to interrupt. This is all very new to me because I'm only just becoming a Christian. I'm not used to church. But I have this strong feeling that God wants me to tell you that you're going to get better.'

3 The miracle lady

An immigrant from South Africa, Wendy Cashmore had not long before been deserted by her husband and was facing the prospect of bringing children up on her own. But for the first time in her life she had found Jesus.

Jen's response to Wendy's hesitant speech was tears. Someone else wrapped up the meeting.

In her electric wheelchair Jen went in pursuit of Wendy. 'Please pray for me, now,' she asked simply.

The young mum, in her twenties, looked horrified; 'Sorry, I couldn't. I really don't know how to pray. I haven't got a gift of healing.' With that she dashed out of the church.

But Jen's wheelchair gave chase. It was not until some hours had passed, however, that Wendy, surrounded by a crowd of women, began to pray in public for the first time. The prayer was simplicity itself; no theology, no thees and thous. As Wendy says, 'A prayer a child might have prayed.' No excitement. There was just a feeling, on Jen's part, that this might be part of a gradual process of getting better.

It was Wendy who had the immediate feeling that everything was all right. Others helped Jen out of her chair. In Wendy's words, 'Somebody passed her her walking sticks. She pushed them away. From what I can remember she just towered. She was so tall . . . .'

With everyone staring, Jen was embarrassed. She ran — yes, ran — to the ladies' loo, and locked herself in. Feeling had returned. She gripped the loo roll.

Her mind couldn't take it in. Later, Tony was 'absolutely confused'. He felt both worried and threatened. Jen didn't know what to say.

The next day was her daughter's birthday. She walked into the kitchen and, to the amazement of the children, began baking the first birthday cake in eight years. The cake turned out uneatable. But who cared? Duncan, then 15, kept saying, 'Mum, you'll fall. Be careful.'

But Jen didn't fall.

'Within days', in the words of Tony, 'we went for a walk in the countryside. I felt so tired trying to keep up with Jen. She was just charging away. I hadn't walked more than 100 yards with her in years, without her being absolutely, totally fatigued. That day I realized that something really different was on.'

'For two months Mum was in a state of euphoria. She'd do things like play music really loudly, . . . ' says Duncan. People *wanted* to be sceptical, but the difference was too obvious. The local paper in Tunbridge Wells covered the story on the front page.

But Jen is emphatic that her healing was not a miracle.

Dr. Gareth Tuckwell is not so sure: 'An individual who's had the results of *viral encephalitis* for eight years would be very unlikely to get up and walk if she'd been in a wheelchair, and especially if she'd had recurrent infection, recurrent trouble.

'What *is* a miracle? *I think a miracle is something that causes us to wonder and points us to God. It doesn't have to be focused on cure.* We're all going to die one day, and the fact that Jen was in a wheelchair for eight years, and was prayed for, and is completely recovered and able to go up mountains and be a mum and live life to the full, for her to give testimony to what God has done in her life, to *me* is a miracle. Whatever the medical explanation, which I can't work out, it doesn't weaken the fact of what God has done in her life.'

Now millions have seen Jen, Tony and the family romping across the fields — Jen fully recovered — in BBC2 and ITV documentaries. Jen's fame before her illness as a children's author had meant that Sir Harry Secombe had interviewed her in her wheelchair on the problems of permanent disability. After the healing, Sir Harry arranged to interview Jen a second time for 'Highway' — on how it felt to be cured.

The question was an obvious one: 'Do you ever feel guilty that you have been healed and others have not?'

Jen says, 'Yes', and confesses that this feeling is especially poignant since, over the last eight years, most of her close friends have been disabled people. But she believes *her* healing has been of *some* comfort to them. 'I talk to my friends who are disabled and I see in them the peace-joy that God gave me. The fact that I am well, they tell me, gives them hope that, when the time comes, they will be well, too.'

Jen is frank about the conflicting views. Some people proclaim a miracle while others talk about 'remission'.

All Jen can testify, day by day, is that she is absolutely and totally well, sound in wind and limb — and that the peace-joy God gave her face down in the mud continues in the daily miracle of a life and body rebuilt.

The folk in the street call her 'The Miracle Lady'.

4 Awkward questions

By the time we interviewed Jen, the healing was three years into the past and her story was available for all to read in *Unexpected Healing* (Hodder).

As we approached the beautiful, four-storey, end-of-terrace house overlooking the park, we noticed the 'For Sale' sign and wondered if all was well. We worried a bit. There were so many questions — even after all the TV programmes and books — to which we still wanted answers. Was it *really* a miracle? How do you define a miracle? How come God heals this person and not that person? Why had half a hundred people with terminal illnesses for whom I had prayed died anyway? OK, so Mike and Paul had been healed — or so it appeared — but how about Iris and Allan and Kevin and . . .

Someone was coming down the stairs.

. . . and how about Marion with all the pain and indignity of MS (in hospital yet again)? And why had Joy, 26 — 'Vivacious, Dedicated, Dearly loved' read her tombstone — had life full of brilliant promise extinguished in a head-on collision at Christmas? Why . . . ?

When Jen Larcombe, with an athletic 5′ 10″ frame and a broad disarming smile, answered the door, we were ready for battle. Full to the brim with awkward questions. Ready to find a flaw in this all-too-well-documented healing.

The Larcombes' many-windowed sitting room overlooking the park is up a steep flight of stairs. Jen took them two at a time. We puffed on after. Before we settled down, we had to be shown where the lift had been. Now the ceilings have been made good, more or less, and there are strategically-placed squares of carpet.

Over tea and scones we looked through the 'before' photographs: the wheelchair-bound, emaciated, disjointed

Jen, and the po-faced family. We hardly needed the 'after' pictures. The vibrant, strapping Jen was beaming in front of us, but it *was* interesting to see the jubilance on the faces of the family. Our favourite photo, taken the day after she was healed, was of Jen holding the redundant wheelchair above her head.

My wife kicked off the questions while I set up the cameras. I was thinking; It would be all-too-easy for this woman to be insufferably pious. After all, *she* has been healed.

It would have been easy for her to adopt a God-has-it-all-in-hand-no-problems approach. But there was none of that. She was all too well aware of the problem of endless, unexplained suffering. She had been on that journey and articulated most of the questions in *Beyond Healing*. But, behind all, there was a sense that she trusted God in all circumstances, no matter what. It was difficult to imagine her without that fidelity. But my wife was learning that in the early stages Jen had been bereft of all things save confusion . . . .

As soon as she had been able to bring her thinking to bear on the problem back in 1982, she had discovered that viral encephalitis is an inflammation of the brain from which many people die. Seventy per cent of those who survive are left with some kind of ongoing damage to the nervous system. She had first panicked, then dropped into depression.

At the very least, there would be scarring to the kidneys and other organs because of the inflammation. Leave alone what would be; the present was bad enough. The inflammation of the nerve casings through the body — as well as the brain — caused scarring of the Myelin sheath of the nerves, producing the symptoms of MS. The resultant incontinence and the inability to feel, grip, smell, taste or see properly had almost destroyed her will to live. *Almost.*

Over the eight years of her suffering, cold and flu viruses had frequently sent her into the intensive care unit of the local hospital. On four occasions her husband had been told that she would not live more than a few hours. Then when, after a couple of months in hospital, and against the odds, she had come home, it had been a case of starting right back from square one. The eight years had brought significant decline.

Repeatedly, Jen insisted that the most important healing had been the one in 1984 — two years into the illness — not the one in 1990. Face down in the mud, Jen had sensed that God was face down in the mud with her. There she had stopped striving, had given up on her desperate doing. It had been a parable of salvation. And, as God gives salvation to those who recognize their helplessness and surrender, so, face down in the mud, Jen had received *spiritual healing*. Thereafter, her relationship with God had been one of trust, fidelity.

The pictures taken, I was lobbing questions at Jen. I wanted her to say some more about reactions to her healing, particularly those of her husband and family.

Jen distinguishes between long-term and short-term reactions.

Long-term . . . .

Janey, an adopted daughter, had been in London for four years and had abandoned Christianity. Since her mother's healing she was at home, working in the precinct and finding her way back to Christ.

Duncan, 17, had had a hard time through the years of his mother's illness. Three or four days after her healing he announced: 'Mum, if God can do this to you, He can do anything!' He has become a committed Christian, whereas previously it would have been impossible to drag him to church.

Sixteen-year-old Richard had learned to love the Lord, too.

Eldest daughter Sarah, 25, and doing her PhD at Oxford, had had her commitment strengthened. With her husband she was about to work full time for the Church.

Younger daughter Naomi, at the University of Southampton, after a negative initial reaction had had her faith strengthened.

And son Justyn was in the Royal Horse Artillery and had had an extrovert commitment to the cause of Christ.

Initial reactions?

Negative, irrational, even hostile. But Jen claims that much of the fault was her own.

She returned from Hazelmere, understandably, in a state of euphoria. Arriving home she mounted the concrete steps to the front door, dragging her wheelchair behind her and looking (her words) 'a bit too militant and triumphant'. The initial response of the family would appear to have been irritation. 'What stunt is Mother pulling now? What new traumas is she about to put us through? It is bound to end in tears.'

'It was a tremendous shock,' said Jen. 'I went off in the morning looking ill — and I *was* ill. They had had to help me to dress, to put my collar on, see I had my tablets with me, and all those things. Then I came bouncing back through the door. Next thing I was climbing up on the table to pin balloons to our high ceiling in preparation for Duncan's party. He was terrified . . . .'

Sarah, though shocked, could see that her colour was different from when she had left home, and realized that something out of the ordinary must have happened.

Richard, 4 when his mother became ill, was 12 then. He said: 'I want my own mum back. I've never known you walk. I can't remember you walking and running like this. I want *my* mum back.' He didn't like the new mum.

Jen admits to having made massive mistakes. She had been immobile for eight years. Suddenly, she was hyperactive. She started going upstairs and tidying bedrooms. Previously the family had looked after her. If she had been sitting down the only way she could get up was by being lifted from under her arms and physically pulled up. 'They had to do so many things for me,' said Jen. 'Suddenly I wanted to do *everything* for myself. I resented anyone helping me to do anything. I would push them off.'

Hardest hit was Naomi. For practical purposes Naomi had been Jen's carer through the eight traumatic years. She said, 'I don't know who I am any more. I feel redundant. You don't need me.' Naomi, 18, had since the age of 10 shadowed her mother everywhere. She would never leave home even for a night in case she was needed. She was emotionally bound to Jen.

'So you see,' Jen concluded, 'it took them all about ten days to two weeks to come to the realization that I was entirely, completely well again.'

And well Jen most certainly was, and is. 'What was so extraordinary was the complete surge of strength and energy. The first day after I came home I got up at five in the morning and I walked till seven. Then I got these awful blisters on my feet because I didn't have shoes that fitted me properly. In the afternoon I went out with my son Justyn, then doing a PE degree in preparation for the army. "Well, Mum," said Justyn, "I think I'm going to work out an exercise regime to get your muscles up." That afternoon', said Jen, 'we went out for this walk round the park in Sevenoaks, and we walked on for an-hour-and-a-half at high speed. At the end of the walk Justyn said, "Mum, I'm not going to bother with that exercise regime. You don't need it!" '

Tactfully — I hope — we pressed Jen to talk about her husband's reactions.

He had coped well with all the emergencies during the eight years of trauma. The marriage had survived because he had made his own space. From time to time he needed to escape and went out on his own of an evening.

How had he reacted to the healing? 'He found it harder than anybody. He's a very quiet, shy sort of man and when he doesn't understand something, or something's worrying him, he pretends it isn't happening. I came home that night and he went off to the allotment and spent the whole evening digging, and then went out to a church meeting. He's an elder at the church. He didn't come home till midnight. He couldn't cope with it. Next day he just went out early in the morning as usual, but came back late. For ten days he would not talk or communicate. He didn't even see me walking. It's hard to believe, but he was terribly worried that it wouldn't last . . . .

'*I* knew I was healed because I'd had three months to get ready for it. But he had not had that adjustment period. He was quite angry that God hadn't told him. I made a specific request to God that, in some way, He would send some sort of message to Tony. This was after ten days. On the next day after I'd prayed that prayer I said, "Now we're going out, and you're going with me. You're going to talk to me." And the two of us went out, and we went over to Southborough, a lovely open stretch of country, and, after we had dropped Richard at a concert, we walked for about an hour. I walked at high speed to show him what I could do, and pole-vaulted over gates and ran up a hill. He came puffing after me, as a man of 46 would! And suddenly, at the top of the hill, he said, "We've got a future, haven't we?" '

The next day Tony gave up his well-paid job as one of Her Majesty's Inspectors of Schools. 'God's done an incredible thing here and we must share it.'

And share it they have, through a variety of means, none of them well paid.

All of which accounts for the 'For Sale' notice outside the tall, end-of-terrace house by the park in Tunbridge Wells. The Larcombes are looking for something smaller.

5 Shouting at God

'When I think about it, I feel terribly guilty that I was healed, and so many are not,' said Jen Larcombe.

Indeed, so many are not healed that books have been written with titles like *Why is God Silent?* and *Where is God Now?* Less than a year before her own healing, Jen Larcombe published *Where Have You Gone, God?*

At times our frustration builds up so that we feel like shouting at God.

The case of Christopher Buckingham affected many Christians like that.

The mental picture I have of Christopher is how I saw him in the intensive care unit of the Queen's Medical Centre, Nottingham. His frail body was a torment of exquisite pain. He was a 5-year-old with the body of a baby, and all he wanted was to be left alone.

The tragedy began three years previously. On a sunny afternoon in Grantham, toddler Christopher was out playing with his friend. His mother, Margaret, noticed that his body was discoloured with an abnormal number of bruises. Leukaemia was diagnosed. Chemotherapy was commenced.

But that laddie was a fighter. More than that. He was one of those children with that little extra something that makes them go over big with everyone. In no time, at least two newspapers were running regular features on his progress. Then he got into some of the nationals.

Christopher's Scottish grandad, Jack Lindsay, was soon giving me daily bulletins. A committed Christian, Jack was praying for his little grandson. At home and at work we prayed for him in morning worship. Most congregations in the town brought Christopher's name on a regular basis to the attention of the Great Physician.

Distraught parents, Peter and Margaret, were advised

that the virulent form of the disease that Christopher had could be helped by a life-saving bone-marrow transplant, conducted in the United States. Vast sums of money were needed. The local newspaper featured an appeal. Christopher's case made the national television news.

The end result of the publicity was that British surgeons conducted the operation at the Royal Marsden Hospital and the £34,000 raised was put into an appeal fund to help other children suffering from leukaemia. Christopher and his mother appeared on Breakfast TV to swell the fund. The boy, barely 5, let slip that he was a supporter of Manchester United. In no time, arrangements were made for the world-famous team to play the local side at Grantham. All in aid of the fund. At the last moment, a cruel hoaxer shattered Christopher's dreams.

Not to be beaten, United Captain Remi Moses arranged another fixture at Grantham. Christopher was to kick off.

But Christopher's condition was deteriorating.

The town's 5-year-old hero was admitted to the Queen's Medical Centre, Nottingham. The crisis came twenty-four hours too soon.

And there we were — doctors, parents, grandad Jack and I — by his bedside. My prayer was urgent.

The town was willing him to live, but Christopher wanted to be left alone. Dad, a big man, was passionately angry. The doctors wanted permission to perform one last operation. Like Christopher, Dad believed there had been suffering enough. The doctors persisted: 'Just one more time . . . . It might be his last chance of survival.'

Dad gave his permission.

Instantly Christopher was wheeled away.

For a long time after that we all sat in a sort of waiting-room.

Despair, extreme anger, and a hope born of desperation

fought for control of the big man who was Christopher's dad.

I tried to say things that might help him. And got nowhere. It was like trying a gear that would not engage.

Every statement, opener or argument I thought of seemed too trite to utter. Words were my business; but every combination of words seemed redundant, even irritatingly trivial. My years of education and what I had considered, till then, to be a fine-tuned theology were of no use in that place. The father was suffering as his boy suffered, and only Someone suffering in the same way could help. So I left it to Him. All *I* could do was listen.

Elsewhere in the Queen's Medical Centre an exploratory lung operation was in progress. Christopher had viral pneumonia. They found seven different viruses in his lungs. He was brought back to the ICU and put on a life-support machine.

The Manchester United match took place. Another leukaemia victim kicked off. Red's captain, Remi Moses, visited Christopher in hospital and left him a Manchester United jersey.

Two days later, Christopher was taken off all drugs to enable him to be aware of his surroundings.

We were still praying hard.

Next day the decision was taken to switch off the life-support machine.

'Christopher only lasted ten minutes after they'd turned off the machine,' his mother recalled. 'Early in the morning he opened his eyes for me and then Peter. We were so frightened that he would suffer at the end, but it was very peaceful.'

It seemed that the whole town turned out for his funeral.

As grandad Jack and I drove back from the Queen's Medical Centre on the crisis day, we had very little to say.

Christopher's pain was just one stab in the pain-wretched human condition — Somalia, Ethiopia, Bosnia, Mozambique — but it consumed our minds and obliterated all else. In common with many Christians, when the news of Christopher's death broke, our over-brimming minds were shouting, 'WHY?'

And the question was shouted at God.

In my boiling brain swirled the notion that it was all part of the outworking of evil in the world, and that God's gift of free will came into it somewhere. I knew that God suffers when we suffer, and then some. I knew that, through ultimate suffering on Calvary, there shines from the unblocked entrance of Christ's tomb the prospect of an ever-lasting world where sin, suffering, injustice and all of the devil's inventions will have no further existence. I knew that there, then, I had to hold on and trust, and urge others to do likewise, to trust, even without understanding.

But what stung above all was that an innocent child had suffered, not been healed, died. That made some of the parson's platitudes in the pulpit appear not only empty, but angry-making:

> 'I walked a mile with Pleasure,
>   She chattered all the way,
> But left me none the wiser
>   For all she had to say.
>
> 'I walked a mile with Sorrow,
>   And ne'er a word said she,
> But, oh the things I learned from her
>   When Sorrow walked with me!'

What could 5-year-old Christopher learn from suffering and sorrow? He was dead. While acknowledging that character and experience are refined through hard knocks, I could not find the answer to the WHY? question.

All through history, men have been asking the WHY? question.

Scottish Reformer John Knox said that he 'never feared the face of man'. Nonetheless, chained up in the galleys he found himself doubting God.

New England Puritan preacher Cotton Mather fled the Old World in search of religious freedom in the New. But in a few short years, as he was peering through a red haze of pain, his faith faltered and he found himself asking, 'Is God really there?'

Martin Luther said that for all of us there are days when faith trembles in the balance and we ask, 'Is it true? Is it true?'

The WHY? question is as old as sin.

There are plenty of Bible writers who echo the WHY? question.

Midianite hordes, like locusts, had been swarming over Israelite land season after season, despoiling cattle and crops. When God sent His angel to commission Gideon to be His champion, the angel said, 'The Lord is with you, mighty warrior.'

Gideon responded with a WHY? question. 'If the Lord is with us, why has all this evil happened to us?'[1]

In his personal agony Jeremiah asked God, 'Why is my pain unending and my wound grievous and incurable? Will you be to me like a deceptive brook, like a spring that fails?'[2]

When the widow's son was dying, Elijah asked, ' "O Lord my God, have you brought tragedy also upon this widow I am staying with, by causing her son to die?" '[3]

Job demanded, ' "Does it please you to oppress me?" '[4]

From the cross Jesus cried out, ' "My God, My God, why have you forsaken me?" '[5]

Always the WHY? question.

The oldest book in the Bible, Job, is devoted to the

question of suffering — because suffering is the oldest question. After Job and his friends had wrestled day and night with the issue, God suddenly said, 'Now answer me this . . .' And He went on to ask Job scores of questions about earthly things. He was saying, 'Look, Job, you don't have the answers to these. How do you expect to understand heavenly things?'

The book of Job does not provide a comprehensive answer to the problem of suffering. But it *does* say that only God has the full picture. It *is* emphatic that suffering is not connected with the sin of the sufferer, but has to do with the larger design, an alien force opposed to God's will for the planet. It becomes evident, by the end, that man has only a fragment of information with regard to the great questions of life, death and suffering; and that the full story is beyond our mental grasp.

Scripture makes it clear that God is big enough to take all our shouting and listen to all our questions. Still more, that when we shout and weep, God is shouting and weeping too.

But put the question baldly, 'Why are some healed and others not?' and I can begin to rationalize, but I do not have the answer. Scripture tells me that if I *did* have the answer, I should have the mind of God. We have to be content to know somewhat less than the Omniscient One. There are times when we simply have to hang on and take Jesus at His word; 'What I do thou knowest not now; but thou shalt know hereafter.'[6]

[1] See Judges 6, especially verses 12 and 13, NIV.
[2] Jeremiah 15:18, NIV.
[3] 1 Kings 17:20, NIV.
[4] Job 10:3, NIV.
[5] Matthew 27:46, NIV.
[6] John 13:7, KJV.

6 Instant solutions

We become most disillusioned with God when disaster strikes close. A child is born with spina bifida. A husband is killed in a car accident. Cancer sets in.

Instant solutions are sought. We want a God who strides into human history on a regular basis and sorts things out.

When we feel this way, we are vulnerable to people who offer just such solutions.

Early in her illness, Jen Larcombe fell prey to such people. Now, she says, 'I'm worried about people who present God with a long agenda; "Lord, you've really got to heal my back" or whatever. For two years I went every place under the sun to get healed. I would not tolerate illness. To me it was a sign of failure. Finding myself ill was insupportable. I really felt that there was some sort of way you could have a miracle if you came at it from the right direction, prayed the right way, went to the right person, forgave everyone — and went through everything.

'I had a whole week of fasting, trying to write down everything that might be "blocking" my healing . . . .

'Disappointment followed disappointment. Each made my illness worse. Now I see this happening with other people; the huge pressure put on sick people by other Christians — *and* by themselves. They gear themselves up to going to some big healing event. And nothing happens.'

Jen has a vast volume of mail — and phone calls — from sick people every day. The day we spent with her she received a six-page letter from a lady who wrote, 'God said through someone He was going to heal me.' She had gone along to a big 'healing rally'. She'd come away still in pain; worse, not better.

The sick and disabled are often manipulated by those

who say, 'God has told me to tell you . . . .' Or, 'I have spoken with God and . . . .'

In the United States, mass-healing services are often televised. Those who conduct them occasionally run summer 'healing crusades' in European cities, including London. Philip Yancey tells the story of a postgraduate theology student who lost his faith over just such a crusade. The crowd had gone wild when a man on stage 'announced that he had been diagnosed as having incurable lung cancer with six months to live — but that God had healed him'. The experience had brought the postgraduate 'certainty of faith'. The importance of the event to him was such that he felt the need to talk to the healed man. After a bit of detective work he found his phone number. A woman's voice answered. The postgraduate asked to speak to the man by name. He never forgot the woman's reply: 'My — husband — is — dead.' Then she hung up.[1]

Dr. Peter Masters, since 1970 minister of the Metropolitan Tabernacle (Spurgeons) in London, is deeply concerned about what he regards as a false form of worship. True worship, he says, is 'intelligent appreciation and adoration of our glorious God'. The new, false worship is, he says, purely subjective, 'for it is all about *my* feelings, *my* moods, *my* health'. He senses a de-emphasis on genuine conversion and views the advocates of the new form of worship — 'the healing crusaders' — as exponents of a variant on the old salvation-by-works theology.[2] Masters is perhaps the most vocal of a growing minority of senior evangelical clergy who are deeply disturbed about any form of worship or ministry dependent on 'signs and wonders such as casting out demons and dramatic healing'. Most are careful to distinguish between the false and the true, contending that the charlatans are merely detracting from the genuine exercise of the gifts of the Spirit, including healing. The false ministry, it is contended, has more in common with occult New Age and 'Christianized' Buddhism than with the religion of Jesus Christ.[3]

Specific, extra-biblical practices are detailed to enable us to recognize the false healing ministry when we encounter it:

☐ when healers make much of possessing a 'personal gift'

☐ when Christians are encouraged to uphold the belief that all have an absolute right to demand and expect healing

☐ when interaction with demons is practised as an aspect of exorcism

☐ when trances or ecstatic states are induced to assist healing

☐ when the sick and disabled are encouraged to believe in the absolute certainty of healing.

Jen Larcombe has real concerns about certain attitudes prevalent within even mainstream Christianity; 'The Church has a real problem . . . . There is a stress on how people *ought* to have enough faith and that if they did have enough faith they'd jolly well get better . . . . They pray for the sick, then give them a little while to get better, and then, if they're not better in, say, a year, they say, "Ah well, they're blocking their own healing." If you can just get your faith-level high enough, you'll be healed.'

Mrs. Larcombe continues; 'It's the Lord who does the healing, not the person. Lots of people pester me to put them in touch with the girl who prayed for me. Very occasionally, I have obliged. But it's not she who healed me, it was Jesus just working through her. And I don't know that she's been used by Him since. Certainly she never had been before. It was He. So really we need to go to Him direct.'

Professor Verna Wright, MD, FRCP,[4] a Christian, has provided a well-researched analysis of the ministry of many of the healing crusaders.

Professor Wright stresses that in a sense all healing is divine; including the healing performed by doctors and surgeons. But she stresses that the suggestion that 'all may be miraculously healed, provided they have sufficient faith', is both unbiblical and dangerous. She is sceptical in the extreme of the long-term validity of healings of the sort conducted by 'mass-healing ministries'.

She describes the visit of an American team to Leeds and how she, with five medical colleagues (Christian doctors), was present to analyse and assess. All 'were so incensed by what they saw that they afterwards wrote an account of their reactions'.

The proceedings began with an hour of repetitious chorus singing. That produced heightened emotional tension and, among the more susceptible, 'reeling and writhing'. At no point in the meetings was the Bible used. There were prayers of confession and repentance and then the exhortation; 'Hold out your hands. Feel heat coming through you. Your eyelids may feel heavy. You may feel like falling; some may scream. It's all right. The power of God is resting on you.'

Those seeking healing were encouraged to describe their symptoms or illnesses. They were then put into a trance. They were told that they would not be unconscious but would hear all that was said to them. While those in search of healing were in the classic hypnotic state, 'amplified voices of team members came through, "Break that bondage. Release their heart. Set them free."'

Professor Wright concludes, 'One of the five doctors was a leading psychiatrist, an expert on hypnosis. He described what had happened as hypnotic trance with suggestions.' Throughout the meetings, says the Professor, 'we saw no change that suggested healing of organic or physical disease. Just the results of hypnosis.'

It is significant that in Jen Larcombe's case spiritual

healing did not come during the two-year period of her frenetic attempts to be healed physically. It came at a time, in fact, when she chose 'to stop pestering God for healing'.

'I believe that we cannot manipulate God by our prayers,' says Jen. 'Actually, being ill is not the worst thing that can happen to us. After those first two years I came to realize that it's Him I needed in the centre of my life, not healing. I'd become problem-orientated. *My* problem, *my* illness.'

We asked Jen; 'What would you say to someone who was wanting healing?' Her answer is a classic; 'We need to come to Him and open ourselves to Him, and say, "Lord, do something with me. Mend me." Then He does what's right.

'You can't earn your salvation — you can't earn your healing. We need to fight the *effects* of illness. But we need to ask the Lord to come into the centre of our lives and to do with us what He wants. We need to be able to accept the fact that He might not, at this time, be prepared to heal us. I know that during the six years from 1984 to my healing in 1990 I learned so many things about Him. They were rich years. Looking back, I wouldn't have been without them. They were blessed years to me.

'I'm sure that when we open ourselves to God, He does what's right. Sometimes He needs to heal us inside and outside. We only expect Him to heal us outside. To us this body is so important. But He sees the inside, the really important part . . . . Spiritual, not physical, healing is the way of salvation . . . .

'God doesn't always take the illness away. We can actually live fulfilled, happy, useful lives in chronic illness, in a wheelchair, in all sorts of problems. It's the resentment and self-pity that is the binding factor. I have learned that you can be happy but ill. I'm in contact with approaching thousands — let's say hundreds for honesty's sake — who have had some kind of accident, have some sort of illness, MS sufferers, those who've had strokes, that sort of thing. Some of them are quite young. Many have come or are coming to terms with their condition. They have progressed from self-pity to something approaching happiness and fulfilment. People say, "Oh, it's just the devil." I'm sure it is; it comes from the devil. But, like Joseph in the Old Testament, you can say, "It was meant for ill; but God meant it for good." You would be amazed at the difference when we can accept it as something that can be "worked together for good".'

In addition to her counselling ministry, and her speaking tours, *and* her tremendous output of excellent Christian books (fact and fiction), Jen, with her husband Tony, runs Hildenborough Holidays. It's a company founded by her father. The holidays are for the sick and disabled; 'They need to get away, and their carers need that, too.'

Jen says we have to reach the point where we can say, 'You're in charge, Lord. I can trust You for everything. People say, "I'm trusting the Lord for healing". But, in fact, we should trust Him for *everything*, not just healing. We can trust Him for illness. Some of the people who have the greatest faith and friendship with God are people who are ill or disabled.'

But having said all that, Jen wants us to understand that God *is* still in the healing business; 'God didn't stop intervening supernaturally with the end of the gospels, or the Acts of the Apostles.'

As Jen spoke, without knowing it she had pulled me up with a jolt. Often it falls to my lot to pray for the sick, sometimes the terminally ill. When doing so, it has been my invariable practice almost to demand total healing, and to do so in the Name of the Father, Son and Holy Spirit. Jen's words made me think of a Christlike, mild-mannered colleague whose equally invariable practice in prayer has been to entrust the sick one to the care of the all-loving, allgracious God. No demands, no agendas. He has it right after all.

---

[1] Philip Yancey, *Disappointment with God* (Zondervan 1988), pages 38 *et seq.*

[2] Peter Masters, *The Healing Epidemic* (Wakeman 1988), pages 10-19.

[3] ibid., pages 21-39.

[4] ibid., pages 202-227. A very different view of certain of the healing ministries is presented in John White's *When the Spirit Comes With Power* (Hodder, revised edition, 1992).

7 Putting God in a box

Not that God always works to the guidelines or fits in with the formulas we work out for His benefit.

Take the time He healed an atheist.

This is one of the cases that I should simply have disbelieved had I heard about it through the media or from some enthusiastic clergyman. As it is, the X-ray evidence at the Walter Reed Hospital, Washington DC, the testimony of the medics involved and the high profile of the man himself makes the case for the divine healing of Major General Lawrence Fuller in December 1973 as close to cast-iron as such cases ever get.

The case was drawn to my attention by Dr. William Shea. Shea, having gained his MD at Harvard, subsequently decided to retrain in the area of archaeology. After mastering the ancient languages and learning to decipher the various types of cuneiform, he did his PhD at the University of Michigan. I once spent a profitable period following Dr. Shea round the main biblical archaeological sites of the Middle East. He is first and foremost a scholar. He never speaks without footnotes!

Major General Fuller, the leading barrister in the US Army, had PhDs in both Engineering and Law. And he was a convinced atheist. 'There are', says Shea, 'two kinds of atheists. There is the pragmatic atheist; the kind of person who really just doesn't want to be bothered with God, pursues materialistic success, worships the almighty dollar or the almighty pound and, if challenged, comes up with feeble excuses for his rejection of God. There is another kind of atheist; this kind of atheist has carefully thought through and regimented his arguments against the existence of God and, in discussion, will be happy to present systematically, point by point, why you should be an atheist too. General Fuller was such a man.'

Fuller retired from the highest legal office in the United States army at the age of 65. During his years in the army, Fuller affirms that it had not really been comfortable to be an atheist; many of the US military are believers of one sort or another. As part of Fuller's retirement procedure at 65, he had to go to the Walter Reed Hospital for a thorough medical checkup. After a week of tests, Lawrence Fuller was called by the senior surgeon into his office to discuss the results. The news was bad. It had been discovered that he had cancer of the colon and required immediate surgery.

Not understanding the urgency of his case, Fuller made plans to go home, arrange his affairs and be ready for surgery in a couple of months. However, the senior surgeon at the Walter Reed said, 'You don't understand. You need to have surgery on Monday.' That day was Thursday.

Fuller got the picture. It was fairly serious. He went home to attend to his affairs. Everything was tied up by the Sunday night and he was preparing to go into hospital the following morning. Understandably, lying in bed, he could not sleep. Though his wife was sound asleep beside him he found himself staring at the ceiling. According to his own testimony, as he stared — he vows he was wide awake, and you can see why he would be — a strange thing began to happen. Before his eyes it appeared that the ceiling was 'pulled back' by a disembodied hand. Much later he would compare that hand with the one Daniel saw writing on the wall at Belshazzar's feast. The hand came down until it touched him right over his sigmoid colon where the cancer was. When the hand withdrew, Fuller affirms, the ceiling closed.

He shook his wife until she awoke. He said to her, 'It's all right. You don't need to worry. Everything is OK.'

Next morning Fuller went into the Walter Reed

Hospital, the chief military hospital in the American capital. He said to the surgeon, 'Look, you don't need to operate. I don't need to have surgery. It's OK. I've been healed.'

The surgeon was used to irrational reactions of that type and assumed that severe stress, resultant from the recent discovery of the cancer, had caused it. It was Fuller's resolute determination to submit to no further medical examination that caused a heated argument with the surgeon. Finally, the two men reached a compromise. The X-rays would be retaken and the colonoscopy (the endoscopic examination of the colon) would be redone. They were. Fuller even submitting to a barium meal. The results? *There was no sign of cancer.* Better than that; the surgeon gave it as his opinion that General Fuller's colon looked as if it was 'as good as new'.

Dr. Shea, who has interviewed General Fuller and the other principals of the case, concludes: 'The testimony to that miracle sits today in the archives of the Walter Reed Hospital X-ray department. The X-rays were taken five days apart on the same patient. The first shows the cancer. The second shows no cancer.'

After his discharge from the Walter Reed Hospital, General Lawrence Fuller had a lot to think about. His mind was forced to grapple with concepts totally alien to his way of thinking. Chief among those was the concept of God. When *The Washington Post* published his story, Fuller had a lot of awkward questions to answer. He had made a lifelong crusade of his atheism. 'What about all those old arguments?' he was asked. His reply: 'They're meaningless.'

The General acknowledged that God had given him back his life. He decided that he owed Him something. He is now a committed Christian and an active member of a congregation at Silver Spring, Maryland.

Why would God heal an avowed atheist, and not heal hundreds of committed Christians of the same affliction, despite thousands of prayers? We can only conjecture. It is part of the will of God for the human race that everyone should have some chance of salvation.[1] Was that the only way God could reach Fuller? Fuller's well-documented healing has become known to millions, including the entire US military establishment. Already his testimony has brought many to Christ. But we cannot say that that was why the healing happened. Millions of miracles would be warranted by the same argument. So many, in fact, that in the end faith would come to depend on exposure to the miraculous. God's *modus operandi* would appear to be based on an economic use of miracles. Indeed, it is clear from Scripture that God prefers faith to be built on a firmer foundation.

Fuller's healing, like that of Jen Larcombe, led to resentment in some quarters. In Jen's case, those who resented her healing were, in many instances, the very people who had rejoiced at the strength with which she had coped with her affliction. Those who resented Fuller's healing seemed to be saying that God was unfair. Indeed, in certain Christian publications some writers came close to the question repeated in Job and the Psalms, 'Why do the wicked prosper?' There was also something akin to Jonah's resentment that, despite his warnings, God spared Ninevah.

Of course, there is a common reaction whenever a healing takes place. Jen Larcombe uses the word 'furious' to describe the response of many 'Christian' people to her healing. In their carefully-worked-out theology, God no longer intervenes supernaturally in human affairs. Such interventions stopped when the record in the book of Acts had been completed. 'We've got doctors now,' they argue. 'We must pray that the doctors will give the right drugs and the right diagnoses; that the surgeons' hands will be guided. But we cannot expect God to intervene in our lives. He doesn't speak to us directly any more. Only through the Bible.'

And that view has much to commend it. The heavens are always silent these days. So many prayers for healing seem to go unanswered. Then, just at the point when all the facts seem to point to God's abdication of His 'direct intervention option' a miracle happens and all the guidelines we have laid down for God's benefit, and the formulas we have worked out both to explain and restrain Him go by the board. We've put God in a box, but, rather inconveniently, He has burst out!

'It says in the Bible that God doesn't change,' maintains Jen Larcombe. 'So why should He stop doing something at the end of the Acts of the Apostles? I believe you can see the hand of God at work all through history. And when that hand intervenes in our country, in our town, in our street — it makes people very angry. And by "people" I mean "Christian people".

'When I wrote up my story, including my healing, in the book *Unexpected Healing*, my GP worked over the manuscript with a fine-tooth comb and let through nothing he didn't approve of. He let it be known that he had done that. As a result, he has attracted some violent criticism, the *most* violent from another Christian doctor. His argument is that I had viral encephalitis and its effects and, therefore, could not have got better. People do not get better from viral encephalitis. This Christian doctor has broadened his attack to other books, including other testimonies of healing, supported by other doctors . . . . He's been vocal in attacks on the people involved in books like mine, investigating every single claim for a miracle, to prove that it didn't happen.'

Of course, behind the attacks on Fuller's healing has been the assumption 'God only helps those who are on the team'. Is this a spin-off from the argument 'God will heal you if you have enough faith'? It certainly reflects the reaction of many Christians when disaster strikes: 'Hey, God, I'm on the team! Why *me*?'

---

[1] 2 Peter 3:9, NIV.

8 Do Christians receive favoured treatment?

When things get out of whack Christians are often the first to yell 'Why?'

The book of Acts. The age when, by common consent among Christians, God was still in the 'direct intervention', miracle-working business. Surely at that time, more than any other, God would exempt the members of His 'team' from the slings and arrows that sliced the air to strike the rest of the human race?

Far from it.

Paul was 'on the team', arguably, 'team leader'! Silas was on the team; and so were Timothy and Luke. In fact, that foursome was doing a good job for God in Asia Minor. Until, that is, God sent a message to Paul that the services of the team were required in Macedonia. [1]

As the four were boating across the Bosphorus, their nerves must have tingled with the excitement of thrilling exploits. From Neapolis where they landed they trekked on down to Philippi. Founded by the father of Alexander the Great, the city was then a major Roman centre and Macedonia's capital.

A few days were spent appraising the situation before they made a start. They were surrounded by superstition and a bitter hatred of all things Jewish. There was a growing antagonism against Christians. But the team felt confident about their mission. God had called them. All would be well.

But God doesn't always organize things our way.

Things started well enough. Lydia was converted and baptized. 'Surely', they must have thought, 'God is backing this venture.' And that's when things went out of whack. A fortune-telling slave girl began to follow Paul around, shouting. After putting up with that 'for many days' 'Paul became so troubled that he turned round and said, "In the name of Jesus Christ I command you to come out of her!" At that moment the spirit left her.'

It was unfortunate for Paul and his companions that certain entrepreneurs saw their profit margins disappear at the point the demon left the girl. In no time they had incited a mob. Paul and Silas (Luke and Timothy must have escaped) were being dragged through City Square before the magistrates. Mob and magistrates joined in trouncing Paul and Silas. The two men were both Jews *and* Christians, so Philippi's prejudices were firing on all cylinders.

Paul and Silas were 'severely flogged'. That meant being tied to a stake while thirty lashes with flint-impregnated thongs were applied to their backs by men with arms like shot-putters. Their backs would be laid open, in ribbons.

Did it occur to them to ask in those days of 'direct intervention': 'God, what are You doing? Where are You? We're answering *Your* call; why this? You haven't even stirred up a decent Roman to see justice done!'?

The gaoler saw that the ire of the populous was on full throttle. Paul and Silas were placed 'in the inner cell' of Philippi's gaol, 'their feet in the stocks'. An armed man 'was commanded to guard them carefully'. That was the time to give up. Right? God had deserted them. It was the inescapable conclusion.

The inner prison was full of the worst offenders. The only sounds would be groaning and cursing. No light, no air, no toilets; a stench to make the stomach heave.

Paul and Silas were fastened into stocks. Their bleeding-ribboned backs lying in the dirt.

There was every ingredient to induce bitterness: 'Lord, WHY? We're on the team. Working under orders — *Your* orders. Are You *really* there? Did You *really* speak? Do You *really* love? Or is there *really* a God? Has this whole thing been an ego trip on our part?'

It would appear that such thoughts never entered the minds of Paul and Silas. 'About midnight they were praying and singing hymns to God, and the other prisoners were listening to them.' Negative thoughts had not entered the minds of Paul and Silas. In chains they were enjoying the freedom of the Gospel. There's a lesson here for *all* Christians, including the ones who believe — totally without foundation in Scripture — that God has provided a copper-bottomed guarantee that trouble will never come *their* way.

'Suddenly there was such a violent earthquake that the foundations of the prison were shaken.' Then the final indignity: to be trapped or crushed to death in that hell-hole. *Lord, where are You?*

'RIGHT HERE!'

'At once all the prison doors flew open and everybody's chains came loose.'

'You came up trumps after all, Lord!'

Darkness, confusion; a brilliant opportunity to escape.

Over the confusion, Paul heard the hard-bitten Roman gaoler. Knowing the penalty he would suffer if his prisoners escaped, he was about to commit suicide. 'Don't harm yourself!' shouted Paul. 'We're all here!'

Lights were called for. A trembling gaoler fell at the feet of his Christian prisoners and asked, 'What must I do to be saved?' Without food for twenty-four hours, having had no sleep, with a bleeding back, in the stench of the prison and shortly after midnight, Paul introduced the gaoler and his family to the Risen Lord whose presence, apparently, he had never once doubted. One obtuse, cold-blooded gaoler was transformed — *imagine what it meant for a gaoler to be a Christian!* — and his two calloused hands were bathing the wounds of the prisoners.

Still without sleep, Paul found that his problems were

not yet over. At daybreak he had to stand his ground against Roman officialdom. And well into the morning, released at last, Paul still had enough left in him to 'encourage' Lydia and the other Christians in Philippi.

To Paul, problems and pain were just another route to a closer relationship with his Lord. From him the Master eclipsed the problem. The problem never eclipsed the Master.

Recounting his adventures at a later date, Paul could recall that the Jews had flogged him five times; three times he had been beaten with rods; once he had been stoned; three times he had been shipwrecked, and rarely had he been away from one sort of danger or another[2] — since, that is, he had been 'on the team'. In all reversals he had heard the voice of Jesus, saying, ' "My grace is sufficient for you, for my power is made perfect in weakness." ' Hence, Paul could summarise his 'on the team' suffering this way: 'For Christ's sake, I delight in weaknesses, in insults, in hardships, in persecutions, in difficulties. For when I am weak, then I am strong.'[3]

There are, apparently, no on-the-team exemptions. But more important than that, there is an assurance. His grace is sufficient. His power — equal to all situations. His person — by your side in the worst of troubles. And the bond between Christ and His followers cannot be dissolved. Paul himself wrote: 'Who shall separate us from the love of Christ? Shall trouble or hardship or persecution or famine or nakedness or danger or sword? . . . No, in all these things we are more than conquerors through him who loved us. For I am convinced that neither death nor life, neither angels nor demons, neither the present nor the future, nor any powers, neither height nor depth, nor anything else in all creation, will be able to separate us from the love of God that is in Christ Jesus our Lord.'[4]

Near the harbour mouth at Whitby, where northeasterly gales whip the sea into a frenzy and appear to threaten the small lighthouse, there is a quotation on the wall: 'You are mightier than all the breakers pounding on the seashores of the world!'[5]

On or off 'the team' our problems are small compared with the power of the living God, our grasp of things tiny by comparison with the infinite brain of the Creator. In Him every believer's life has aim, direction, purpose and pattern. Problems will come, but with the problems will come both the power and the presence.

---

[1] This account is taken from Acts 16:6-40, NIV.

[2] 2 Corinthians 11:24-29, NIV.

[3] 2 Corinthians 12:9, 10, NIV.

[4] Romans 8:35-39.

[5] Psalm 93:4, Living Bible.

9 Suicide at Hell's Mouth

But perhaps the Christian, though expecting no special privileges, who has not doubted the power, person and presence of God is the exception.

Despite every avowal of faith, when problems strike it is all too easy for the problem to eclipse God — and, with Him, every positive thought.

There was a suicide at Hell's Mouth.

I arrived there shortly after it happened.

It was weird.

Only weeks before, I had taken the midnight express out of King's Cross. Between tunnels the train juddered from 80mph to a screeching standstill. 'Another jumper!' announced the guard. We had to wait until ambulance men and police had completed their grisly work before the journey could continue. The following day I discovered that in the previous decade there had been 3,370 such suicides on British Rail.

But that night, darkness provided an effective shroud.

At Hell's Mouth it was all done in the grey light of a drizzly day.

Hell's Mouth is a wide bay on the North Cornish coast between Portreath and Godrevy Island. Here the great, unchecked, Atlantic breakers thunder against a vast, sheer rock-wall. Over the centuries, scores of ships have come to grief here and been broken up by the might of the savage ocean. As we arrived, the driver of a newish white car had chosen to drive at speed across a cliff-top car-park and hurl himself and his vehicle hundreds of feet down into the immense clouds of spray and hissing spume below. So far below, in fact, that it took a very long lens to enable me to see, for sure, that the mangled metal could contain no living person.

In the inquests and coroner's courts convened in the weeks thereafter, the story unfolded.

It was a simple one.

The young car-driver had been jilted.

I thought of Jen Larcombe's eight years of trauma — pain and disability increasing almost daily — and of her cheerful determination not only to hang on to, but make the most of, life.

Then there was Marion and her MS; wheelchair-bound, a mechanical device to haul her into bed, then the long hours before daybreak in which she was unable even to turn herself. But Marion manages mostly to be cheerful; fills her days with friends, interests and activities; and fixedly hangs on to life. Her husband cut and ran years ago.

And Alan! Alan had — of all things — been a theology lecturer. A brain tumour had been diagnosed. There had been chemotherapy and prayers for physical healing; but, in a series of operations, surgeons had removed more and more of his brain. Before his death, one half of his head was bandaged over. But, blessed with a lovely wife and family, Alan had fiercely clung on to life, cheated Death of its prey as long as he possibly could.

A person whose life is threatened clings on to it with all his force.

And then there is the fact that suicides, when they occur, occur only in the prosperous countries of the West. Even here suicide is a phenomenon of the haves, not the have-nots. Suicide is a rare, almost unknown thing in the Third World.

Apparently, the people worse off still think that there's a great deal of good in their trouble-filled world and pain-wracked lives.

There's something to learn here.

It revolves around the problem of good.

Of course, it's the problem of evil that hogs the headlines every time.

If you believe that God is a God of love you have one problem to account for: the problem of evil.

If you *don't* believe in a God of love, you have millions of problems . . . .

For every thousand people who raise the question, 'Why is there evil?' there's not a single, solitary person to raise the question, 'Why is there good?' And yet 'Why is there good?' is by far the bigger problem.

William Paley wrote, 'Whoever made us and our world could have made all our senses to minister constant pain to us. But, instead, He has made all our senses to minister joy. If it were not so, why is not every sound a discord, every sight ugly and every taste bitter? Why?'

The 'normal' of life is nightly rest, daily food, the ordinary use of our many faculties and the unhindered enjoyment of our lives. The greatest blessings of all exist in profusion. But, because they *are* the norm, the *unremarkable*, they are not the stuff of which headlines are made. The *ab*normal — death, disease, disaster — makes better headlines.

The news is so full of the abnormal that our minds become conditioned to think of it as normal. Hence our lifeview and the questions we ask are built on that assumption. When BBC newscaster Martyn Lewis asked if it would be possible for the news team to feature one item of *good* news each day, he was met with derision by the other members of his profession. Senior BBC newsman Peter Sissons was quoted as saying that to report good news would not be to report reality.

Sissons was, of course, wrong. By 'reality' he meant the variations from the norm that make news. Virtue, fulfilled lives, healthy people, loving families, incident-free air travel, disasterless holidays — you've got the idea! — do not make news copy. It is in the nature of the media and of our sensation-seeking selves to accentuate the negative and eliminate the positive.

Calamity, loss and heartache grab our attention because they are the exceptions to life. It is the testimony of Jen, Marion and many like them that every life is crammed with mercies, regardless of the pain.

If you believe that God is love you have one problem: the existence of evil. If you don't, you have a million problems. You have to explain beauty, truth, friendship. You have to explain why there is so much love in the world, and so many altruistic relationships, friendships, comradeships, that lift us above every stress and strain.

If there is no God of love there are so many things we have no way of explaining. Take the miracle of design, for example. Everyone knows about the cornea, that transparent covering of the iris in the eye. Did you know that it is the only part of the body that does not have blood vessels? Consider what it would be like if that transparent part of your eye — the clear bit on the outside — had blood vessels like the rest of the body. It would be like peering through a latticework. It has been said that every cell in the body contains more facts than there are in the *Encyclopaedia Britannica*.

Then there is the miracle of fertility. Why isn't every seed like a stone? Why in every tiny acorn is there generation after generation of forests of oaks? Why?

Yes, Christians have to wrestle with the problem of evil. But non-Christians have a million more problems.

Then consider the immutability of law. But for the fact that the universe is based on 'the rule of law' that causes pain, life would be unbearable, a nightmare, a continual tragedy. A little child falls out of a ten-storey window; the law of gravity destroys her. But what are the alternatives?

Suppose that *you* had the specific gravity of lead at one moment, and of thistledown at another . . . . Suppose that carrots grew up, and cabbages grew down . . . .

All worthwhile things now existent depend upon the reliability of natural law. Without it there would be no agriculture, no science, no life. Many of the problems that exist represent the flip-side of necessary natural law without which life would be insupportable. God is, apparently, a God of law. He has made a *universe* and not a *multiverse*. Though, from time to time, for reasons beyond our comprehension, He may choose to intervene, setting aside natural law. This is what we call a miracle. But, in the main, the atoms march in tune — according to law. And that law is ultimately for our good and for our blessing.

We are woven together into families and friendships. Whatever affects one member of the family inevitably affects all. Of course God need not have made it like that. We could all have grown up, independently, like trees. But God invented family and friendships to maximize our happiness. And so, when one part suffers, the rest suffer. Parents suffer more when their children suffer than when they suffer themselves. The question is: Would you get rid of filial love, conjugal love, the love of friendship, in order to get rid of pain? I think not.

When audiences are asked, 'Has most of your pain come from things of nature or from *human* nature?' in almost every case they will confess that approximately four-fifths of their pain comes from *human* nature, from people. God did not invent swords and long-bows, bayonets and H-bombs, germ warfare and intercontinental ballistic missiles. Man did. God did not create robots; He created men and women with freedom to choose. As a result of the choices man has made, he has inflicted pain on himself and on others. Many of the so-called natural disasters — megafamines, floods — ecologists are now discovering are just some of the side-effects of what man has done to the planet; the erosion of the ozone layer, earth-warming, shifting weather-patterns, and the rest. Further, in all Western countries the top six killer-diseases are diseases of choice; the results of eating too much, and of the wrong stuff, and of moving too little. It has been estimated that in Western countries three out of four people die of heart-disease or cancer; and the causes of over 90 per cent of both are known. For every one committing suicide on the midnight express or at Hell's Mouth, so to speak, there are countless millions in prosperous countries committing suicide by knife and fork.

It is the widespread acceptance of universal natural law, including freedom of choice, that, even in the pampered West, makes what happened on the midnight express out of King's Cross or at Hell's Mouth a rare exception to the norm of life.

There are still plenty of suffering Christians who, like Jeremiah in the midst of *his* sufferings, can say: 'Because of the Lord's great love we are not consumed, for his compassions never fail. They are new every morning; great is your faithfulness. I say to myself, "The Lord is my portion; therefore I will wait for him." ' Lamentations 3:22-24, NIV.

10 God's great risk

Of course, at the exact point when we're up against it, we might wish that God would gatecrash natural law a bit more frequently for the benefit of us and ours.

Then, when the awfulness of one of the planet's open wounds is borne in upon our thinking, we cry out, like John in Revelation, ' "How long, Sovereign Lord, holy and true" '[1] — do You permit this, and this, and this? Every Christian has prayed that prayer.

So why *are* the heavens silent?

Why *does* God permit this planet to be a university of hard knocks?

More than anything else, I wanted to lead Kelvin to Christ. But there was so much in his background he could not come to terms with. His earliest recollections were of his father's brutally beating his mother. Then, as he had grown in awareness, he had grasped that his fast-living father was flaunting young, glamorous women in front of his bruised and tearful mother. While his mother might have felt some sense of relief when his father left, Kelvin felt that he, personally, had been deserted. That had bred bitterness, and that bitterness had, in some way, brought on a new generation of sorrows. During the months when I first came to know Kelvin, it was difficult to put down his failures in the job market to anything other than discrimination. It seemed that all the world was against him, and that God was no great help. That was before his wife left him for someone else, taking with her their 3-year-old son.

As Kelvin dug into his Bible to find answers, he found himself far more at home with the mental picture he had built up of the God of the Old Testament than with the suffering Saviour, Christ, to whom I was seeking to introduce him.

Kelvin wanted a God who intervened *instanter* to right wrongs and punish offenders. In something near exasperation, I recall saying, 'Kelvin, your God is more like a *capo mafioso* who happens to be on *your* side. Someone like Robert Louis Stevenson's John Amend-all but with unlimited power — not excluding access to laser-zapping techniques.'

'Now *that* would be my kind of God,' replied Kelvin with enthusiasm. 'If God were to do *that*, the whole world would wind up in His camp. Why doesn't He?'

Of course, at no point in history did God ever act in a way that would entirely have met with Kelvin's approval at that stage in his experience.

But there was a period when He came close to it. It was the period between the commissioning of Moses to lead the Exodus, and the anointing of the first King of Israel. All told, I suppose, God's experiment in detailed, almost daily, intervention in human affairs lasted about 500 years. God was self-evidently fair, deafeningly audible and symbolically visible.

From Sinai God laid down a comprehensive legislative structure, covering every area of life, and provided a system of rewards and punishments acknowledged as fair. The pillar of cloud (or fire) and the urim and thummim meant that God was giving directions as and when required. God was far from silent *then*. Indeed, at times, He seemed to shout. Rebellious Korahs, Dathans and Abirams *were* devoured.[2] Nadabs and Abihus *did* encounter their deserts.[3]

But what effect did 'direct intervention' have?

New Testament writers looked back on that period — 'the Old Covenant' — as demonstrating the incapability of man to fulfil a contract with God. They used it as an argument for the need of a New Covenant, one based on God's forgiveness and grace.

God's noisiness and interventionism notwithstanding, the Israelites found every which way to flout His comprehensive legislative programme. Reading the account of the forty years' wandering around the Sinai peninsula, I find it difficult to avoid the conclusion that the newly-liberated Israelites were acting like children, whinging and whining, despite dependence on a daily miracle to provide them with food and drink.

When God took stock at Kadesh Barnea, it was clear that 'direct intervention' had not brought the Israelites to spiritual maturity. That was so massively evident that God decided to start again — with a new generation. The old generation who had lived through the ten plagues of Egypt, crossed the Red Sea on dry ground, drunk water from a rock, been fed by the daily miracle of manna, *and* listened to God thunder from Sinai, were spiritual dwarfs. They had every proof of God's existence and favour that it was possible to ask for, but what good had it done them? Instead of their responding with love and worship, the fear they harboured produced open rebellion.

Is this account contained in Scripture to explain why God rarely goes for the 'direct intervention' option these days?

Spectacular miracles do not, apparently, build faith. Nor, on the other hand, do they produce atheists. But God does not want that kind of belief. He is looking for a different kind of faith, a faith that signs and wonders can never produce.

After the anarchy of the period of the judges, God spoke to His people through prophets. Through the messages of men like Isaiah, Jeremiah and Hosea we receive a picture of a God who wants to love and be loved. In Hosea, in particular, the picture is of a God deeply hurt by the unfaithfulness of His people. The lens is demisting; clearer contours are beginning to show through. The picture is one of a God heartbroken by sin and the calamities the people have brought upon themselves.[4] At the end of the seventy-year exile, we hear God saying to the vulnerable band about to set off back to a rubbled-over Jerusalem, ' "Can a mother forget the baby at her breast and have no compassion on the child she has borne? Though she may forget, I will not forget you! See, I have engraved you on the palms of my hands." '[5]

An overview of the Old Testament leads one to a profound truth. The people who related to God best — Abraham, Moses, David, Isaiah, Jeremiah — were those who treated Him like a Friend, a Father, a Counsellor. This is a profound truth because it gives an insight into God's angle on things. In sickness or health, triumph or disaster, joy or sorrow, this is the relationship God wants to have with us. And the essence of the relationship has to be that we want to relate to God in this way — by choice. *Free choice.*

And it is with this free choice that any understanding of God's relationship with man, and of suffering and death and disaster, has to begin. Soren Kierkegaard said: 'Man is God's risk . . . . God has, so to speak, imprisoned Himself in His resolve.' The sovereign God taking risks and imprisoning Himself? Philip Yancey takes the view that in His creation of man and woman God approached that kind of astonishing self-limitation. His plan was not to create a planet in which all beings would be overwhelmed by His overpowering presence. He wanted them to be free, free even of Him. Free to love Him, or not to love Him — not programmed to adore Him for ever.[6]

In fact, God has been in the risk-taking business for a long time.

He created the heavenly hosts. No problem. But He gave them *free will* and took the risk of being hated,

slandered and defied — or loved for what He is. Hence —
paradox that we can never fully understand — evil began in
the mind of a being *in heaven*. Revelation 12:7-9 recounts
the origin of evil and Satan's expulsion from heaven. Verse
4 infers that a third of the angelic host were expelled with
Satan. In both Isaiah and Ezekiel — Satan in the role of
'the King of Babylon' and 'the King of Tyre' — the issues
which originated Satan's rebellion are clarified.[7] Jesus Himself said (Luke 10:18, RSV), ' "I saw Satan fall like lightning
from heaven." ' His words had an immediate application:
seventy of His followers had returned triumphant, having
cast out demons in His name. His words also represented an
historical statement. Jesus — the Christ who had existed
from the beginning (John 1:1) — was recalling the great
inter-galactic conflict back in the mists of pre-history and, in
His mind's eye, recalling the fall of Satan and his hosts.

With sin already abroad, God created Earth. Great. But
then He took risks. He didn't declare it off limits to the
fallen host. He gave the beings He made to people the earth
free will and took the risk of being hated, slandered and
defied — or loved for what He is . . . .

This puts the fall of man in context. From Genesis to
Revelation we encounter an anti-God force of great power
and cunning. He is arrogant and determined, and the
originator, through sin, of all disease and disaster; the im-
placable foe of God and man who is out to spoil all that is
good and lovely. We find him in the Garden of Eden at the
beginning of the story. We find him in the lake of fire at
the Bible's end.

The prophets clearly present evil as the direct result of
man's using his free will to make wrong choices. But the
more powerful picture is of One who would come to free
man from the consequences of his choices — disease, death,
disaster, injustice — and from sin itself.

To use Kierkegaard's word: God took the greatest 'risk'

in sending Jesus. The sovereign God was to imprison Himself in human flesh. The essence of man's freedom was made evident; The sculptures could spit at the Sculptor; the characters in the play could rewrite the inlines.

God dared to come in Person into the sin-choked atmosphere of the Silent Planet, the camp of the enemy. Coming, not as a Cosmic Commander with a space fleet at His back, the ultimate Time Lord; but as a Baby, unable to protect Himself from malign influences from the outset bent on His destruction . . . .

Kelvin ultimately came to realize that the 'direct intervention' he had longed for was best accomplished, not in the Sinai mode, nor in the words of prophets who provided a part of the answer and an outline of the picture. He grasped that God does not want *any*one — let alone *every*one — in His 'camp' through fear, but free choice.

Kelvin now believes that the ultimate in direct intervention was when God came in the Person of His Son, Jesus. Through the suffering Saviour he once despised, Kelvin has found healing for his memories and for his life.

Commenting on the problem of suffering and the coming of Jesus, Kelvin says: 'Now the time had come, not just for an answer, but for a solution . . . .'

---

[1] Revelation 6:10, NIV.

[2] Numbers 16:23-33.

[3] Leviticus 10:1, 2.

[4] See Hosea 11.

[5] Isaiah 49:15, 16, NIV.

[6] Philip Yancey, *Disappointment with God* (Zondervan, 1988), page 60.

[7] Isaiah 14:12-14; Ezekiel 26-28. See Michael Green, *I Believe in Satan's Downfall* (Hodder, 1981).

11 Why doesn't God *do* something?

It's an old question.

They asked it in the Old Testament.

Abraham *must* have asked it.

Had God outlined His plan to Abraham? It seems likely. Abraham was to leave the advanced, opulent city in which he lived and trek hundreds of miles to a land God promised him. There he would commence a sort of pioneer settlement; and from it would grow a nation as numberless as 'the sands of the sea'. Through that nation God would seek to restore the fallen world.

Abraham was so enthusiastic about God's plan that he set off immediately. But, having revealed the great enterprise in a blaze of direct revelation, God went silent on Abraham. And God *stayed* silent for years and years. At 99, with a wife aged 90, Abraham must have been asking, 'Why doesn't God DO something?' for a very long time.

The post-Sinai years of 'direct revelation' were preceded by a 400-year period in which God had been silent and, apparently, inactive.

In the age of the prophets God was certainly active; but the age of miracles would appear to have been limited to the ministries of Elijah and Elisha. They were not prototype prophets. Nor did the miracles God worked through them cause more than the very briefest of religious revivals. After the biggest pyrotechnic display of all, Elijah was on the run for his life. And it was during that on-the-run period that God revealed His preferred method of communication to His prophet; not pyrotechnics, nor wild tempests — but whispered words of wisdom. Prophets like Isaiah, Hosea, Habakkuk, Jeremiah, Ezekiel, used no striking displays of supernatural power; the power of words had to suffice.

Psalmist Asaph voiced the WHY? question. 'O God, do

not keep silent; be not quiet, O God, be not still.'[1] Other psalmists were equally urgent; 'O Lord, you have seen this; be not silent. Do not be far from me, O Lord. Awake, and rise to my defence!'[2] 'Why, O Lord, do you stand far off? Why do you hide yourself in times of trouble?'[3]

The prophets themselves echoed the 'Why doesn't God DO something?' question. Jeremiah; 'O Hope of Israel . . . why are you like a stranger in the land?'[4] Habakkuk; 'How long, O Lord, must I call for help, but you do not listen? Or cry out to you, "Violence!" but you do not save? Why do you make me look at injustice? Why do you tolerate wrong?'[5]

Accused of inactivity, God did not argue. Through Isaiah, Jeremiah, Ezekiel, Zechariah and the rest, God detailed the injustices and calamities that were happening as a result of man's wrong choices. God outlined what the *right* choices should be, and what consequences would ensue from making those choices. At times God was emphatic that His restraint was an interlude of mercy. The prophets had mistaken mercy for aloofness.

Then, 400 years after Malachi's vision of a time beyond time when all wrongs would be righted, Jesus came.

Did people stop asking 'Why doesn't God DO something?'? There seemed to be something approaching a consensus among those who saw God in Jesus that He was doing all the wrong things.

Among those who have examined the record of Jesus' healing ministry, there have been many critics. Augustine asked that, since Jesus had the power to heal, why had He not healed everyone? Since He had the power to raise the dead, why were only three dead raised?

When Jesus failed to measure up to expectations, His contemporaries killed Him. God-with-us notwithstanding, they still cried out, 'Why doesn't God DO something?' Jesus reserved one of His strongest put-downs for people demanding 'signs and wonders'.[6] Satan provided Jesus with three short cuts to achieve his Messianic goals; the sort of exhibitions of miracle-working power Kelvin was sure would recruit *everyone* for 'God's camp'. When we say to God 'DO something!' are we presenting Him with the same short cuts with which Satan tempted Jesus?

Jesus could have called down heaven's battalions to subdue Jerusalem. Instead He sat on the Mount of Olives and wept as He foresaw the consequences of a city's wrong choices. C. S. Lewis expressed clearly the confusion behind the 'DO something' demands we make of God; 'Perhaps we do not realize the problem, so to call it, of enabling finite free wills to co-exist with Omnipotence. It seems to involve at every point almost a sort of "divine abdication".'

When we hear of man's latest inhumanity to man we're outraged and demand: 'Is God uncaring or impotent?'

But it's fair to ask a question of ourselves: Precisely *what* do we expect God to do?

We're driving home. We hear fire engines rushing towards our street. We pray, 'God, don't let it be *my* house.' Think of the implications. If, for example, you have left the iron on and the house has caught fire . . . . Think of the flip-side of the prayer: Let it be somebody else's. Remember, God has set up a universe, not a multiverse. Is it fair to expect Him to change the rules when we get in a jam? Thalidomide causes defects in the foetus. Should we blame God for not preventing the 'thalidomide babies'? Much hurt comes to us from the actions of other people: rape, robbery, murder. Do we have an inalienable right to God's protection? No; but we still cry out, 'God, why didn't You DO something?' In the backs of our minds is the idea that God runs a protection racket, that we have paid our dues and that, in consequence, we want fail-safe protection!

Occasionally, God does supersede the laws of nature.

Such moments are miracles. Of necessity they are rare, or the universe would dissolve into anarchy. A parent learns much about God's ways of dealing with people. This is especially true when his offspring are living through the adolescent years. Does he let his son make his own decisions, and bite his tongue — or try to stop him? Typically, he learns the pain of watching his fledgling offspring make mistakes as they test their own wings.

God is our heavenly Father. He loves us intensely and wishes the best for us. But He respects that freedom. He will not thrust Himself upon us, crowd us, even though He knows us better than we know ourselves.

The story of the Bible from Genesis to Revelation is the story of the God who limits Himself out of regard for human freedom. No one will be dragged, kicking and screaming, into His eternal kingdom. Because He is love, He seeks freely-given human responses to His love. Because love can be wooed, but not compelled, God has made us free — free to choose Him and free to go our own way. Remember the risk factor?

But to those who shout, 'Why doesn't God DO something?' with the implication that He is always inactive, let's remember that the Bible shows us that He poured out all heaven on our behalf. *God has done something;* in the Person of His Son, at infinite cost, the cost of His life. [7]

'Instead of crushing the power of evil by divine force; instead of compelling justice and destroying the wicked; instead of making peace on the earth by the rule of a perfect prince; instead of gathering the children of Jerusalem under His wings whether they would or not — He let evil work its will while it lived; He contented Himself with slow, unencouraging ways of help essential; making men good; casting out, not merely controlling, Satan . . . .

'To love righteousness is to make it grow, not to avenge it . . . . Throughout His life on earth, He resisted every impulse to work more rapidly for a lower good . . . . '[8]

Nevertheless, in the light of the miracles recorded in the gospels — including the feeding of a crowd the adult male contingent of which numbered 5,000; ordering at least three dead people to life; reducing a calamitous storm to calm — it would be preposterous to accuse God-in-Christ of inactivity!

But the attitude of Jesus towards His own miracles makes an interesting study. His evident pre-occupation was to down-play them. As eternal God He knew too well that even the most dramatic display of 'signs and wonders' does not foster faith.

But the ultimate answer to 'Why doesn't God DO something?' is not in the miracles He performed. It is in the life He lived and in the death He died.

---

[1] Psalm 83:1, NIV.
[2] Psalm 35:22, 23, NIV.
[3] Psalm 10:1, NIV.
[4] Jeremiah 14:8, NIV.
[5] Habakkuk 1:2, 3, NIV.
[6] Matthew 12:39; 16:4; Mark 8:38.
[7] See Philippians 2:6-11; Romans 8:32; John 3:16.
[8] George MacDonald, *Life Essential: The Hope of the Gospel* (Baker, 1971), page 24.

12 The suffering of God

Dietrich Bonhoeffer was hanged by the Nazis in the concluding days of World War II.

In the prison camp, Bonhoeffer had seen man at his most inhumane. To him, what he was witnessing was the last chapter of man's fall; what happens when men give themselves over entirely by choice to the power of evil. Having witnessed unspeakable atrocities, he left these words on his bunk: *'Only the suffering God can help.'*

Elie Wiesel survived Auschwitz. He told the story of a boy whom the SS suspected of sabotage. Along with two men, the boy was hanged. 'The three victims mounted together on their chairs. The three necks were placed at the same moment within the nooses. "Long live liberty!" cried the two adults. But the child was silent. "Where is God? Where is He?" someone behind me asked. At a sign from the head of the camp the three chairs were kicked over. There was total silence throughout the camp. On the horizon the sun was setting . . . .

'The two adults died instantly but the child was so light that he remained alive for half an hour. Behind me I heard the same man asking: "Where is God now?" And I heard a voice within me answer him: "Where is He? Here He is — He is hanging here on this gallows." '

'I feel God has let me down,' I have been told on countless occasions by people struck by a calamity they feel God should have prevented.

Anyone feeling 'let down' by God should pause at Gethsemane and see Him betrayed, forsaken by His friends; 'Then everyone deserted him and fled.'[1] They should pause in Pilate's judgement hall — His lacerated back, the thorn-crown, those whom He had healed and helped and encouraged crying, 'Crucify Him!' And they should pause at

Calvary. Roman nails, square in section, hammered through His wrists and feet. The hideous instrument of torture with Jesus upon it — this King of Truth, not of this world — elevated into the perpendicular and savagely jolted into the socket prepared for it in the rock-face. Searing pain, indescribable agony, horrible, raging thirst, the feeling of suffocation . . . . Upturned faces, grotesque with hate and scorn. Snarled defiance. 'He saved others,' they hissed. 'He cannot save Himself!'

No miracle was worked to save Jesus. If anyone had the right to feel 'let down by God', He did. God was silent. And, in the words, 'My God, My God, why have You forsaken Me,' the desolation in His human heart was made audible.

And why did He have to die?

This is the message of Scripture:[2]

His hands were pierced for the wrong things our hands have done. His feet were spiked for the wandering paths our feet have trod. His brow was thorn-crushed for the wrong thoughts our minds have harboured. His heart was broken for the wrong things our hearts have loved. His side was spear-riven to prove once and for all that the way to God's heart is wide open.[2]

He was paying the price of sin.

In the beginning, God had given man freedom of choice because He is that kind of God. Man had made wrong choices. Sin had blighted the planet and all those who lived upon it. The penalty of sin was death. Jesus — completely God, completely Man — had lived without sin. And He died, not as a martyr, but as a sacrifice. Through His sacrifice, all men and women in every age can choose Him as their Champion and find pardon, peace, joy and the assurance of salvation. Through God's strange transaction, when we accept Jesus as our Saviour our sins are placed to His account, while His perfect life is placed to ours.

'What on earth is God doing for heaven's sake?'

demands the preacher. 'Why doesn't God DO something?' demand the people.

God *has* done something about the evil in the world. It cost the life of His Son.

The good news rings from almost every page of the Bible: in countless ways God cares deeply and passionately. And not only about the world situation; but about the problems and crises in each individual life.

Nobody forced Judas, Caiaphas, Pilate and the rest to do what they did. At Calvary, Satan thought he had won. But Jesus cried out in triumph as He died. God had worked together for ultimate good. If anyone had any doubts about that, they vanished on Easter morning. The heart of the human problem is the problem of the human heart. And God has worked a solution to that problem: hearts are broken and lives changed at Calvary; and the change persists as long as we maintain our day-by-day relationship with the Man of Calvary.

Back to Pilate's judgement hall. Jesus was wearing the purple robe and the thorn-crown. His trial was almost over. Pilate had repeatedly announced that he could find no basis for a charge against Jesus. Then he was questioning Him for one last time; 'Where do You come from?' An unfathomable fear had gripped his heart as, for the first time, he had heard the phrase 'Son of God'. There is no reason to doubt the seriousness of his question.

But Jesus had answered questions enough. Panicky now, Pilate snapped: 'Do You refuse to speak to me . . . ? Do You realize I have power either to free You or to crucify You?'

Note the answer that Jesus gave; it applies as much to you as it does to Him.

' "*You would have no power over me if it were not given to you from above . . . .*" '[3]

And in those final words from the Prisoner about to be led out to die there is precious peace. If I could only hold on to them when death stalks my distant vision and pain

needles my present; when my motives are misconstrued and
my character is assassinated in the house of my friends;
when trouble strikes like lightning and 'Why me?' jumps
out of my mouth — again; when evil's outworking comes
too close and faith falters . . . . *Then my God would always
eclipse my problems, instead of my problems eclipsing my
God.*

What do those words mean? Nothing can happen to a
follower of Christ that has not been filtered, *sifted* through
the love, mercy and grace of the Sovereign God. God's
grace *is* sufficient. Sufficient in sickness and in health, in
joy and in pain, in life and in death.

God cares. Why does He care?

☐ Because each one of us is made in His image. That
is why Jesus, the supreme revelation of God, was always
caring for individuals; the lovely and the unlovely, the lost
and the lonely, the sick and those whose lives were spoilt by
sin. Everyone was of infinite value to Him. Everyone was
made in the image of God. In Jesus, God came close. The
torn curtain in the temple was a symbol of that new
closeness. Jesus offers a long, slow look at the face of God
and says, ' "Anyone who has seen me has seen the
Father." '[4] In the words of Archbishop Michael Ramsay; 'In
God is no unChristlikeness at all.'

☐ He wants us to be His friends. We only truly reflect
God's image when we remain on terms of close personal
friendship with Him. It is because so many have moved
away from God that our society today is dehumanized.
That's why *our* relationships are often in a real mess, because our relationship with *God* is in a real mess.

Three young boys were once boasting about their
fathers: 'My dad is a teacher. He makes me clever for
nothing.' 'My dad is a doctor. He makes me healthy for
nothing.' 'My dad is a clergyman. He makes me good
for nothing.' Scripture makes it clear that we are all
'good for nothing'[5] — until we come to Christ.

☐ He wants to maximize our joy here and save us for eternity. The heart of the human problem is the problem of the human heart.[6] The man who sets out to change society is an optimist. The man who sets out to change society without changing the individual is on a hiding to nothing. Mariette Corrigan, who once began a peace movement in Northern Ireland, said: 'The great problem in Ulster is not political or religious. It is the root of bitterness in people's hearts. You may have political changes, you may have religious changes. But until the root of bitterness is dealt with, nothing is fundamentally changed.' Carl Jung wrote, 'It is becoming more and more obvious that it is not starvation, not microbes, not cancer, not horrendous weapons of war, but man himself who is mankind's greatest danger.'

☐ Through Calvary all things are possible. In some Old Testament books — Job, Ecclesiastes, Lamentations — there is outrage and a kind of bleak despair. We do not find this in the New Testament. The New Testament writers were convinced that Jesus had changed the universe for ever. 'If anyone is in Christ, he is a new creation; the old has gone, the new has come! All this is from God, who reconciled us to himself through Christ and gave us the ministry of reconciliation: that God was reconciling the world to himself in Christ, not counting men's sins against them.'[7] 'For God was pleased to have all his fullness dwell in (Christ), and through him to reconcile to himself all things, whether things on earth or things in heaven, by making peace through his blood, shed on the cross . . . .'[8] 'That power is like the working of his mighty strength, which he exerted in Christ when he raised him from the dead and seated him at his right hand in the heavenly realms, far above all rule and authority, power and dominion, and every title that can be given, not only in the present age but also in the one to come.'[9]

New Testament writers wrote those words, fully aware of

the power of the Roman Empire, its wars and its tyrants, conscious of the prevalence of evil in the world and that, at any moment, they themselves might be arrested and subjected to humiliating torture and excruciating death. To them none of that mattered; through the death and resurrection of Christ, evil had been vanquished and the triumph of good and God was assured.

At times the evil power may seem to be triumphant. But behind the outworkings of evil, and the doings of men, the agencies of the All-Merciful One are at work. At D-Day the devil had been beaten; that was the message of the cross and the empty tomb. And with D-Day past, V-Day cannot be far distant.

In conclusion . . .

God was hurting on Calvary. He continues to hurt when we hurt. Because He is the Omniscient One, He suffers far more profoundly than we do.

A student missionary sees a leper and is touched and genuinely sympathetic, feeling some pain. But then he can go to his room and remove the man's leprosy from his mind. He cannot suffer as the leper does, feeling not only some physical sensations, but also the loneliness and ostracism, the loss of dignity and self-assurance. But God can and does.

'Few give thought to the suffering that sin has caused our Creator . . . . As the "whole creation groaneth and travaileth in pain together" (Romans 8:22), the heart of the infinite Father is pained in sympathy. Our world is a vast lazar house, a scene of misery that we dare not allow even our thoughts to dwell upon. Did we realize it as it is, the burden would be too terrible. *Yet God feels it all.'* [10]

This is a profound statement with regard to the nature of God's love. He is not only with us in all of our sufferings, as the Bible repeatedly promises. He feels as we feel, hurts when we hurt — only more so.

Elie Wiesel was right when he said, 'God is there,

hanging on the gallows.' *Not* because God is dead. But because God endured that hanging.

As we look to Jesus, look in faith, we see Him hurting with our hurt; see the Lamb slain in the funerals of our friends, slain when motives are misconstrued and characters assassinated, slain in every victim of every catastrophe — Ethiopia, Somalia, Bangladesh, Bosnia — slain in every vile deed and ugly word.

But we have a Father who is Sovereign over all. All evil must pass through the sieve of His love and wisdom before it can strike us — *and then be forced to work together for our good*. His love is not sickly sentimentality. It is strong love; the strong love of a parent who is determined to seek his children's good, even at the cost of their pain and his own. God wants a relationship of trust, fidelity, with us in which we can develop, grow. The main obstacle to this relationship is self in a thousand ugly manifestations. Self-indulgence, self-glorification, self-seeking, self-assertion, self-will, self-pity, self-love. If the chief goal is that all-important relationship and the chief obstacle is self, will not strong love use the sieve to allow the 'chastening' that will be to our benefit?[11]

Can we say, 'God will bring good out of this ill thing' — *and mean it*?

---

[1] Mark 14:50, NIV.

[2] Isaiah 53; 2 Corinthians 5:21.

[3] John 19:6-11, NIV.

[4] John 14:9, NIV.

[5] Romans 3:23.

[6] John 3.

[7] 2 Corinthians 5:17-19, NIV.

[8] Colossians 1:19, 20, NIV.

[9] Ephesians 1:19, 20, NIV.

[10] E. G. White, *Education* (Pacific Press, 1903), pages 263-4. Italics ours.

[11] See Revelation 3:19.

13 Bitter or better?

So is there a sense in which suffering can work out to our benefit?

Yes. But if you happen not to be suffering don't be too glib about this one. The parents of Christopher Buckingham — the 5-year-old who died of leukaemia — and *anyone* suffering from a painful illness could be excused for screaming at smug Christians parroting 'All things work together for good to them that love God'. And the God who hurts when we hurt, is on the side of the screamers, not the smug Christians!

Whether we emerge from life's hard knocks better for the experience may well depend upon the attitude we adopt towards them.

One attitude is illustrated by Samuel Clemens, better known as Mark Twain. His childhood was spent in grinding poverty, his family constantly on the move. By the time he reached 15 one of his brothers and one of his sisters had died. At the age of 20 he discovered that his hair had turned white when another brother was burned to death in a steamboat explosion on the Mississippi. He married; and his first child died soon after birth. His own thoughtlessness killed his second child; he put her pram out in the snow, failed to cover her and she died of pneumonia. His carelessness nearly caused the death of his third child: he let go of the pram at the top of a hill. His favourite daughter died when he was away on a lecture tour. Another daughter died of an epileptic fit.

On a number of occasions Twain pointed a revolver at his head, but never found the courage to pull the trigger.

Before his death he wrote a bitter, terrible book and in his will indicated that it was to be published after his funeral. It is unnerving in its fury and bleakness; its hatred of life, faith and God.

Now let's look at John Donne, the seventeenth-century poet-preacher. Circumstances militated against his success in his first two chosen career ventures, and the Church was chosen in desperation. He was ordained in 1615 and a year later his wife died, leaving him with seven children. From 1621 to his death in 1631 he was Dean of St. Paul's. Not long after that appointment, Donne displayed the symptoms of the bubonic plague. (His modern biographers tell us that it was 'merely typhoid', but *he* didn't know that!) The terrible illness dragged on and on, weakening Donne and bringing him to the point of death. Convinced he was on his death bed — no energy, no books, only quill and paper — John Donne wrote *Devotions*. It is, perhaps, the most moving and incisive manuscript ever written about suffering.

At first Donne looks back on his life and tries to make sense of it; after years of meandering he had finally found a way of serving God and, at that time above all others, had caught the plague. The prognosis? A hideous, painful death.

The poet-preacher looks for meaning in it all. Through an open window, he hears church bells tolling and wonders if his friends have acted rashly in anticipation of his death. Then he realizes that the bell is tolling because a loved neighbour has died of the plague. In *Meditation XVII*, inspired by the bells, he writes the wonderful passage commencing: 'No man is an island . . . ; therefore never send to know for whom the bell tolls; it tolls for thee.' He goes on to express the certainty he has in a God who will, beyond the death of death, make all things new and 'bind up all our scattered leaves again for that library where every book shall lie open to one another . . . '. A time beyond time when all mysteries will be made plain and all wrongs righted.

In his 'Hymn to God in my Sickness' Donne writes:

'Since I am coming to that holy room,
Where, with thy choir of saints for ever more,
I shall be made thy music; as I come
I tune the instrument here at the door,
And what I must do then, think here before.'

In his suffering, John Donne held on to Calvary as to a rock:

'We think that Paradise and Calvary,
Christ's Cross and Adam's tree, stood in one place;
Look, Lord, and find both Adams met in me;
As the first Adam's sweat surrounds my face,
May the last Adam's blood my soul embrace.'

Donne declined to be intimidated by the prospect of death:

'Death, be not proud, though some have called thee
Mighty and dreadful, for thou art not so:
For those whom thou think'st thou dost overthrow
Die not, poor Death; nor yet canst thou kill me . . . .
One short sleep past, we wake eternally,
And Death shall be no more: Death, thou shalt die!'

In his *Devotions* the poet-preacher more than hints that he has latched on to an inkling of the good that can emerge from this most devastating of illnesses; 'I need thy thunder, oh my God; thy music will not serve thee.'

When we are in pain, or distress, we shout at God. Does it ever occur to us that God may have permitted the pain and distress as a means of shouting at us? That certainly occurred to Donne. In a later century it occurred to

C. S. Lewis. In his book *The Problem of Pain* (1940) he wrote of 'pain, the megaphone of God'. It was in the minds of both Lewis and Donne that present suffering was an aspect of this transitory world that, experienced positively, could be turned to advantage in preparing them for a better world to come.

Thousands travelled for miles to listen to Donne's sermons at St. Paul's. In them he often harked back, expressing the view that the periods of greatest pain and distress in his life had been the periods of most rapid spiritual growth. Repeatedly he took the view that suffering had purged sin and developed character, taught him total dependence upon God, cured him of worldly ambition. Donne had begun his *Devotions* with prayers that the pain be removed. But the direction of his prayers changed; he began to pray that his pain be redeemed, that he be 'catechized by affliction'.

'*I need thy thunder, oh my God*': For the remainder of his ministry, Donne taught thousands to view pain and even poverty as a means to spiritual maturity. In his suffering Donne believed God had been shouting at him because he had been unheeding of the 'still small voice'. When we cannot be wooed by God's 'music', does He resort to 'thunder'?

'God whispers to us in our pleasures, speaks in our conscience, but shouts in our pains,' wrote C. S. Lewis.

Can we learn something from the radically different way in which Twain and Donne perceived pain? It can make us bitter or better. It can sour us or sensitize us. In the same way that there is nothing good that, if wrongly used, cannot bring pain and evil, so there is nothing evil or tragic which, if positively experienced, cannot bring good and blessing. Everything has two handles; we can decide which handle to take hold of. Pain and suffering are inevitable; but misery is optional.

Suffering made Mark Twain bitter. It made John Donne better. Suffering will come. What will it do for you? What will it do for me?

The older Christian writers — Augustine, Thomas Aquinas, Martin Luther, John Calvin, John Donne and John Bunyan — all accept pain and suffering as aspects of the 'refiner's fire' and potential agents for good. By contrast, twentieth-century Christian writers have been preoccupied with the question, 'How can a loving God permit pain and suffering?' Their answers have been various: some abandoning God, some redefining God, some redefining love. Can we afford to abandon the insights of those who wrote about pain before the discovery of antibiotics and anaesthetic?

14 The mystery and mastery of suffering

C. S. Lewis published *The Problem of Pain* in 1940. At that time he little knew what vicarious pain was ahead in his own life.

Having watched his recent bride, Joy Davidman, die of cancer, he wrote another book, *A Grief Observed*, an outpouring from his grief-stricken heart. In it he said less about pain as God's 'megaphone'. Analyses are not helpful when we are in the depths of despair. He wrote of times of utter desolation, his need desperate, 'when all other help is vain'. Often, he wrote, in those circumstances, it seemed that a door had been slammed in his face and that he had heard the sound of bolting and double bolting on the other side, and after that, silence. His earlier confidence had been shattered to such an extent that *A Grief Observed* was published under a false name.

His comments on 'getting over it' in *A Grief Observed* are memorable: 'Getting over it so soon? But the words are ambiguous. To say that a patient is getting over it after an operation for appendicitis is one thing; after he's had his leg off is quite another. After that operation, either the wounded stump heals or the man dies. At present I am learning to get about on crutches. But I shall never be a biped again.' (Page 43.)

In a BBC radio interview, Lewis confessed, 'You never know how much you really believe anything until you are stretched to breaking point' and 'it becomes a matter of life and death to you'.

But even in that extremity of desperation Lewis did not lose his grip on the belief that God had built two great principles into His creation: a universe run on *natural law*

and *human freedom*. And that, by committing Himself to
those two principles, God had allowed for the possibility of
their abuse. Even in his deepest trough, Lewis acknowledged that God could only be held responsible for the suffering in the world in the indirect way that a parent who
gave his child a pair of roller skates could be held responsible for his fall. There was, he acknowledged, something
wild, unpredictable, savage, about man — and that God was
far more distressed than we are capable of being over the
suffering and injustices which have resulted from that
savagery. In consequence, a 'Condemned' sign hung above
the earth, and in a judgement and restoration — promised
and prophesied — every crooked way would be made
straight. Man did *not* belong on this pain-wracked earth.
It was *not* 'the best of all possible worlds'. This side
of eternity there would always be questions for which there
were no adequate answers. But Lewis was prepared to
wait.

There are times when the suffering is too intense for us
to view it at the time as 'the megaphone of God'. That
phrase may even have haunted Lewis as he watched his wife
die of bone cancer. Nevertheless, looking back, it is possible
for us to see that experience as the seismic change in
Lewis's growth to spiritual maturity. Marooned on a mutinous planet, he thrust out his hands and held on to heaven
by the hems. But his grasp became stronger. God's grace *is*
sufficient. Even in her pain, every 'get well' greeting seem-
ing like a taunt, his wife had been able to assure him of
that. God's grace *is* sufficient to meet the direst of human
needs. Perhaps she, like John Donne, was 'tuning the instrument at the door' in order to make heavenly music.

Psalm 22 — so poignant a parallel of Calvary —
describes the terrible sufferings of an innocent victim.
These sufferings are physical, mental and spiritual. There
is no neatly-formulated answer to the problem of suffering

in this psalm. But to the Christian it brings a fourfold assurance:

☐ *An assurance of the faithfulness of God.* It begins with the question echoed by Jesus on Calvary; 'My God, my God, why have you forsaken me?' But only to the cursory reader is this a cry of unrelieved despair. The Psalmist's feelings are in mutinous disorder, but his faith rises up against his feelings. His opening assertion that he has been God-forsaken denied his feelings: '*My* God . . . .' This psalm centres around a paradox; In the midst of his sufferings the Psalmist *feels* himself God-forsaken, but his faith asserts itself *against* his feelings and lays hold on the faithfulness of God.

☐ *An assurance of the loving discipline of God.* God *disciplines* those whom He loves; and in disciplining us God is treating us as His children. God is not a feeble Father who indulges all the wishes of His children. But in this psalm emerges as a parent whose strong love seeks His children's best good, even at the cost of their pain and His own.

☐ *An assurance of the triumph of God.* Psalm 22 begins with what appears to be a cry of anguish but ends with what is, without doubt, a song of praise. It begins with expressions of God-forsakenness and ends with a triumph of deliverance. In suffering, the Christian has this assurance: However dark the night may be, the dawn is sure to break. Disease and death are not going to have the last word. In the New Testament, Paul, who had a daily encounter with suffering, wrote: 'I consider that our present sufferings are not worth comparing with the glory that will be revealed in us.'[1]

☐ *An assurance of the sympathy of God.* The Psalmist affirms that God suffers *with* us. Psalm 22 was fulfilled in every particular in the crucifixion of Jesus. '*My* God . . .' was not a cry of despair; He believed that God had not finally abandoned Him. But it was a real cry of dereliction as He 'was pierced for our transgressions . . . crushed for our iniquities' that 'by His wounds' we might be healed.[2]

In an Easter sermon at All Souls, John Stott began with these words; 'The Bible is the Word of God but, at the same time, it is a supremely practical book. It does not, however, claim to solve all riddles. For example, there are many references to suffering and to evil. The Bible is full of evil men who prosper and good men who suffer; but the Bible's purpose in examining these themes is not to explain the origin of evil or the meaning of suffering. Rather, it is to help us to endure suffering and overcome evil. The Bible is more concerned with the *mastery* of suffering than with its *mystery*.'

Suffering is the universal lot of mankind.

What differentiates the Christian is his response to it.

This response is not a stoical fortitude, nor is it bitterness: The true mastery of suffering lies with those who even in the midst of it can say, '*My* God'.

My God is, apparently, a God who cares, cares enough not to leave us alone in our self-indulgence. Cares enough to risk our hostility by disciplining us, raising His voice when His whispered words of wisdom are not heard. Cares enough to suffer for us, bearing our sin and pain. Cares enough to suffer *with* us when we are hurting. And it is in this knowledge that *God* is suffering with us that we can find the secret of the *mastery* of suffering.

---

[1] Romans 8:18, NIV.
[2] Isaiah 53:5, NIV.

15 Is God unfair?

They stoned Stephen to death. As he died, heaven shone from his face and he said, 'Lord, don't blame them for this.' One witness of that atrocity was changed by what he saw and heard. In turn, that witness, Paul, went up front in the shock troops of Christianity who changed the world.

One consistent theme of Scripture: God as the expert in bringing good out of bad situations.

Jesus was tempted for forty days — '*If* You are the Son of God . . . ' — and we read of just three characteristic temptations. But, through those temptations, Jesus can help men and women with *their* temptations — *and* He came from the wilderness of temptation 'filled with the Spirit'.

The same verse that records that John the Baptist was put in prison continues 'and Jesus went into Galilee, proclaiming the good news of God'.[1] John's mouth was shut; the mouth of Jesus was opened. From prison John sent the message, ' "Are you the one who was to come, or should we expect someone else?" '[2] But Jesus turns doubt into glorious light. He says, in effect, My argument is not in manuscripts, it is in man: The blind see, the lame walk, the lepers are cured, the deaf hear, the dead are raised and the good news is preached to the poor.[3]

A lawyer tried to start a quarrel with Jesus by asking an awkward question. Jesus turned it to good by telling us the wonderful story of the Good Samaritan.[4]

The pious people and churchgoers found Jesus surrounded by prostitutes and other social outcasts and tried to

spread scandal about Him; 'This man receives sinners.' But
Jesus made the very words of scandal themselves proclaim
the central truth of the Gospel. He then used the opportunity to explain that central truth in a way that nobody could
misunderstand by telling the stories of the Lost Coin, the
Lost Sheep and the Lost Boy.[5]

And then there was Calvary.

The devil thought he had won. Thought that God was
beaten. Thought that man's only chance of salvation was
out of the window for good and all. But Christ's torn flesh
became His glorified body, His crown of thorns became a
crown of glory, the crucified Malefactor became the Saviour
of the world, and Good Friday gave way to Resurrection
Sunday.

But before the triumph over temptation there were forty
days of vulnerability, hunger, loneliness.

While the end of John's ministry meant the beginning
of the ministry of Jesus, John's imprisonment and execution
was a monumental miscarriage of justice.

Before the decisive answer of Jesus, there was the sting
of John's doubt.

The pious people who slandered Jesus, in the main,
turned their backs on His Gospel. They were responsible
for the conspiracy that led to His crucifixion. They in-
stigated the policy that led to the martyrdom of so many of
His followers.

Although Paul was converted, Stephen stayed stoned.

Is life unfair? Is *God* unfair?

For many years now I have woken up each morning to

'Prayer for the Day': 6.25 am BBC Radio 4. Of the hundreds of short talks I have heard, the one that sticks in my memory was an unscheduled one. David Winter, then the head of religious broadcasting, broke into someone else's series to give a talk of his own.

It was the day after the Hungerford massacre. A quiet country town, with people going about their usual summer afternoon pursuits, had suddenly turned into something like the set of a horror film. In the space of minutes a maniac slaughtered many innocent people before turning his gun on himself. 'For some who have survived,' said Winter, 'life will never be the same again. It all seems so utterly pointless and hopeless. And it's at a moment like this, perhaps, that we need to turn again to a great picture of hope, like this one in the twenty-first chapter of Revelation.' And the BBC reader read Revelation 21:1-5. The new heaven and the new earth . . . God dwelling with man on a re-created planet . . . no more injustice, tears, death, mourning, pain, 'for the old order of things has passed away'.

David Winter's tone was uncharacteristically impassioned, urgent: 'There *is* healing, and there *is* hope, though those things lie in the future rather than the present. God does care. He is not indifferent to our tears, our pain, our mourning. Where was He in Hungerford yesterday? He knelt beside the victims. He supported the rescuers. Where is He this morning? In the intensive care unit, at the bedside, holding the hands of those who are bereaved. We do not have an indifferent God. And there's more: One day this whole order of things, this suffering world of violence and passion, will pass away and be replaced by something totally new . . . .'

Life *is* unjust. The *outcome* of the conflict between good and evil was decided on Calvary; but the conflict goes on until God ushers in His new creation.

We live in a war zone. And as long as we live in a war

zone there will be injustice, casualties, heartache, pain, hunger and death.

What had the people who died in Hungerford done to deserve such an appalling fate? Nothing. Evil and its symptoms are indiscriminate.

Jesus made this clear. Pilate had butchered a group of Galileans even as they worshipped. Jesus asked, ' "Do you think that these Galileans were worse sinners than all the other Galileans because they suffered this way? I tell you, no!" ' Eighteen died when a tower in Siloam fell on them. Jesus said, ' "Do you think they were more guilty than all the others living in Jerusalem? I tell you, no!" '[6]

In Hungerford, Galilee, Jerusalem and the 101 trouble spots in today's world: There is no question of justice or fault involved. In the words of David Winter; 'Violence and accident are, sadly, a part of the fallen world in which we live. Very often the innocent suffer. But that answer of Jesus — that stern denial that such events are retribution — came from the Man who died on a cross. He knew what He was talking about. There, indeed, the Innocent suffered. There, indeed, violence did its worst.

'But in the end it was defeated: not by *more* violence, not by hitting back, but by the power of love.'

'Lord, look with mercy on the suffering of Your children. Take away the old order of violence and despair. Bring in Your kingdom of mercy, love and peace. Amen.'

Job is the Bible's case study of a man suffering unfairness, caught in the midst of the war zone. Job's friends based their arguments on the fairness of God and sought to rationalize Job's plight.

Job himself was caught in a crisis of faith. His strident message of life's unfairness seems peculiarly suited to our pain-wracked century. The evil and hedonistic appear to prosper while the innocent die. Job's wife urged the option: 'Curse God and die!' And in our unjust, war-zone world many have taken that option. Jerzy Kosinski and Elie Wiesel, to name but two, took that option during the holocaust.

Others, like Rabbi Harold Kushner, drew another conclusion: God was frustrated, even outraged, by the planet's injustice. Unlike David Winter, however, Rabbi Kushner believed that God could not and would not change the natural order. He abandoned the 'Day of the Lord' concept, fundamental to Scripture; there would, he believed, be no kingdom of God in which justice and righteousness reigned.

Philip Yancey in *Where is God When it Hurts?* and *Disappointment With God* argues persuasively: Do not confuse 'life' with 'God'. Life, argues Yancey, may be unfair, but God is not. Of the thousands he interviewed in preparation for his books, the testimony of one man stood out in the mind of Yancey; 'If we develop a relationship with God *apart* from our life's circumstances, then we may be able to hang on when the physical reality breaks down. We can learn to trust God despite all the unfairness of life.'[7]

External reality can seem to present God as the enemy. Abraham, Joseph, David, Elijah, Jeremiah and Daniel, the Old Testament worthies, could have perceived God as the enemy and roundly berated Him for being unfair. But they did not, though His silence disturbed them. Each one held on to trust in Him despite every hardship. Life is *not* fair. In the words of Philip Yancey, 'The cross demolished for all time the basic assumption that life will be fair.'

While, in argument, Jesus does not appear to have tackled the question, 'Is life unfair?' in life He unquestionably did. Nowhere did He deny life's unfairness. His most scathing words were reserved for the hypocritical and for the rich who abuse their power. When He encountered the sick He was 'moved with compassion' and healed them. Jesus offers flesh-and-blood proof about how God feels about unfairness. He Himself took on physical reality at its unfairest.

Yancey argues, 'It occurred to me as I read the gospels that if all of us in His Body (the church) would spend our lives as He did — ministering to the sick, feeding the hungry, resisting the powers of evil, comforting those who mourn, and bringing good news of love and forgiveness — then perhaps the question "Is God Unfair?" would not be asked with such urgency today.'[8]

When famine hit Jerusalem, Paul did not rail at God for His unfairness. He went on a fund-raising enterprise around the churches he had founded, in order to meet the needs of the starving in Jerusalem.

Down in a Roman dungeon Paul did not scream 'Unfair!' at God. Nor, it would appear, did he demand that God supply his material needs. He did, however, write to his friend Timothy asking for clothing and books. After his trial, without a trace of self-pity, Paul told Timothy: 'At my first defence, no one came to my support, but everyone deserted me. May it not be held against them. But the Lord stood at my side and gave me strength . . . .'[9]

Between the call of Moses and the end of the theocracy God spoke directly, adopted a hands-on approach. But His voice engendered fear, not friendship, and soon it was ignored.

In Jesus, God came in the flesh. And, for three decades, spoke in a human voice that combined authority with extreme sensitivity. But one voice can easily be silenced.

The Church is the body of Christ. The voice that speaks through it, however, is the Spirit's voice, the most intimate voice of all. God's stand against injustice in today's world must be through a Spirit-led Church. Hence above all people Christians should be preoccupied with justice in the world. They are God's hands and, yes, perhaps His voice. Their task is to heal the sick, cleanse the lepers, bring sight to the blind, feed the hungry, condemn injustice — and urge that injustices be redressed. And part of that gospel of hope is 'the day of the Lord', the *denouement* of history when, in the most audible and most visual event of human history, Jesus will intervene directly to end the old order for ever and to establish a new order that will last for all eternity.

---

[1] Mark 1:14, NIV.

[2] Luke 7:18, 19, NIV.

[3] Luke 7:22.

[4] Luke 10:25-37.

[5] Luke 15.

[6] Luke 13:1-5, NIV.

[7] Philip Yancey, *Where is God When it Hurts?* (Marshall Pickering, 1991); *Disappointment With God* (Zondervan, 1988), page 49.

[8] Ibid., page 185.

[9] 2 Timothy 4:9, 13, 16-18.

16 What God wants from Christians

If the Church is the Body of Christ, and Christians are the hands, feet and voice of God in a suffering world, what does God expect of Christians?

First it should be stated that, once again, God is laying Himself open to misrepresentation. In his analysis of the methods of the mass healing ministries, Dr. Peter Masters exposes the cynicism and lack of success of those who believe they can manipulate God by manipulating man.[1] God is not 'on tap', 'on demand', 'at our disposal'. He is a source of limitless strength to those who communicate with Him. But His primary aims are our salvation and our spiritual maturity. Spiritual healing is urged above physical healing.

When, through prayer, we knock at God's door, He's ready to receive us with open arms. But He is not ready to be manipulated by us. Some people would be very happy if God was always at their disposal, ready to act as and when they desire. They would relegate God to the cupboard, or the attic. When they had need of Him, they would go and fetch Him. As soon as He was of use, they would pull Him out of the cupboard. They want God to be usable.

The Lord does not lend Himself to this sort of game. He is a Person, not an object. He is an individual, a free agent. God wants us to respect His freedom of action. We do not tolerate coercion; but sometimes we try to exercise an intolerable control over God. God has the right to reply as He sees fit, by the channel which is most appropriate and at the time that He considers opportune. His wisdom is without limit and only He sees the full picture; only He knows what our best good is.

When we pledge ourselves to a day-by-day relationship with God, we take a certain risk. And the implications of this risk must be accepted in their entirety.

Suppose you receive a letter from someone to whom you do not wish to reply immediately; you may well have good reason for delay. Would you accept that a third party should pressure you into changing your mind? Certainly not! You wish to reserve the right to choose. Your silence, in itself, conveys a message.

What does God want to communicate to us by His silence when He does not appear to respond immediately to our prayers?

☐ God invites us to consider Him as a Person and desires that our relationship with Him should become rich, full of life, and of the unexpected. He knows best; He desires that we respect His freedom of action.

☐ God wants us to be still, as, at times, He is still. We are too frenetic, too agitated. God wants us to enter into His peace. His voice continues to be a 'still small voice'; a voice not audible when our lives are lived in a febrile atmosphere crowded with stress, noise and clamour. God wants us to hear when He speaks to us. Otherwise, how can He confide?

☐ God invites us to think of role reversal. We want *Him* to respond; He may be waiting for *us* to respond. God has taken the initiative in establishing the dialogue; our prayer is a response. God has given us His 'yes' once and for all in Jesus Christ. In Jesus, God has given us everything; and yet we complain that we have received nothing from Him! God's heart is the heart of a Father; ever open, ever warm, ever receiving, ever desiring our best good. His great heart will be moved by our situation, even if He is silent at the time of our petition.

☐ Sometimes when God is silent He is seeking to give us a free hand. He is taking us seriously, standing back and demonstrating trust in us. His silence is not a sign of desertion. Rather, it is a sign of respect. He respects our freedom and appreciates it when we shoulder our own responsibilities. God does not expect us to wait for 'instructions' or 'providences' at every touch and turn of our lives; we are no longer children to be molly-coddled.

Jennifer Rees Larcombe learned these lessons and reached this God-concept during the eight years of suffering that preceded her miraculous healing. From her experience detailed in her three wonderful books — *Beyond Healing* (1986), *Where Have You Gone God?* (1989) and *Unexpected Healing* (1991) — we learn more about God than about Jen. And the God who emerges from her wonderfully-crafted pages is a God who can be trusted and who wants to trust us.

☐ In her first two years Jen had to learn to give up on her frenzied search for stage-managed healing; to abandon all attempts to manipulate God.

☐ After two years of suffering she learned a lesson of immense value and, as a consequence, received a gift far greater than physical healing: she learned that God was hurting with her, suffering every indignity; she surrendered her broken life to Him — and received spiritual healing.

☐ In the six years of suffering that remained, consciously or unconsciously, she learned to put herself in third place: God, others, self. Great as her problems unquestionably were, she set out in a deliberate attempt to share with others the truth that there can be triumph, peace and joy in the worst of adversities — and that there are practical ways of coping.

☐ In her day-by-day relationship with an all-loving, all-gracious Heavenly Father, she grew into trust and fidelity; with patience and peace she waited, with God, for the opportune time.

☐ When the fullness of God's time came, He chose to work through the simple prayer of a new Christian: no fanfare of trumpets — that is not God's way.

☐ Jen's total healing has merely served to make her ministry more active, more effective as it combines practical help for the sufferers and an insight into the loving heart of a God who *can* be trusted.

God seeks to bring us all, whether sick or well, to the relationship of fidelity He established with Jen. A relationship in which we will accept that there are a thousand and one questions that will never be answered until we meet God face to face. And this relationship is often developed during God's silences. In His relationship with Abraham, Isaac, Joseph, Job and David there were many silences. But as they developed their relationship based on fidelity they became friends of God. And all turn up in the Hebrews 11 gallery as 'heroes of the faith'.

The point of the experience of each of them was that in the face of events in the visible world they had to learn to hang on to the truth that in the invisible world was an unseen God who represented righteousness, truth and justice. God listens to our shouts of complaint and questioning; He wants us to know that in our hurting *He* is hurting. Job did His share of shouting — and God would have been the last Person to have blamed him — but he hung on to one conviction: 'Though he slay me yet will I trust him.'

That was fidelity.

Rabbi Abraham Heschel has written: 'Faith like Job's cannot be shaken *because it is the result of having been shaken.*' God's silences can — through prayer and Bible study — be used as opportunities for spiritual growth. Growth towards 'fidelity'. There is, apparently, no greater way that we can express our love to God.

For the Christian, the fount of this love is Calvary.
There Jesus — every external circumstance against Him, and
an immense gulf separating Him from His Father — dem-
onstrated the ultimate example of the relationship built on
fidelity. Both in Gethsemane and at Calvary, in a profound
and mysterious way, God Himself learned what it means to
feel God-forsaken.

To reach fidelity, Job had to hear but ignore the false
theologies of his friends. He externalized much anger and
doubt, but found that God was big enough to hear and to
forgive. When the trauma was finished, Job knew that far
from his being betrayed or abandoned by God his experience had been shared by Him. Learned, too, the real ident-
ity of his enemy, Satan, the initiator of suffering and
disaster. And, even as Job suffered, God had indicated
through His question to him, that through the Fall man's
vision is limited; that if man cannot grasp the facts of the
physical universe he had better leave the workings of the
spiritual universe to an infinite Mind. Job's response?
'"Surely I spoke of things I did not understand, things too
wonderful for me to know."'[2]

It's worth remembering that Job spoke those words
while he was still sitting on his rubbish heap covered with
sores, and *before* his losses had been made good. He had
caught sight of the unseen world, and in its light all his
urgent questions faded away. The real battle had ended
when Job refused to give up on God. In the face of the
sophistries of Eliphaz, Bildad and Zophar, and the urgings
of his wife, Job had affirmed:

> ' "Oh, that my words were recorded,
>   that they were written on a scroll,
>   that they were inscribed with an iron tool on lead,
>   or engraved in rock for ever!" '

Clearly, Job was building up to a climax:

' "I know that my Redeemer lives,
    and that in the end he will stand upon the earth.
    And after my skin has been destroyed,
    yet in my flesh I will see God." ' [3]

Job's most urgent desire, in all of his troubles, was that
he should be allowed to plead his case before God. When,
eventually, the Lord answered Job, He did not directly explain why he had been called upon to suffer. Apparently,
God wanted Job to understand that his greatest need was a
more trusting relationship with Himself. When God spoke
'out of the whirlwind', [4] He seemed to be saying: 'Because I
created this universe, including the world with all its forms
of life, and because I rule over all and control the relationships that exist among living creatures, why should you
doubt My capacity to control the affairs of your life? Take
My word for it: Your vision *is* limited. Trust Me!'
    Our world is full of angst, alienation and pain. It is like
Job's life *before* God spoke to him out of the whirlwind. We
suffer from no shortage of alternative philosophies and
theologies; Job's comforters are in plentiful supply. But in
contrast with Job's friends who misrepresented God, most
modern philosophies are atheistic and many modern
theologies demolish belief in a powerful, loving God. Like
Job we are called upon to exercise faith with no certainty.
Faith that cannot be shaken because it is the result of being
shaken. In the words of Paul Tournier: 'Where there is no
longer any opportunity for doubt, there is no longer any opportunity for faith either.' This is the childlike faith —
fidelity — that is God's gift and the reason why Jesus said
that those who enter His kingdom must do so 'as little
children'. [5]
    This childlike faith is found in surprising places. When

freedom first came to Russia, Jim Zachary, of Russian descent, went to the city of Lvov to bring Christ to a population schooled in atheistic Communism for seventy years. An airline pilot came to his first meeting and listened to his prayer. He decided to try prayer for himself. He was only half serious when he said to God, 'Look here; if You want me to attend these Christian meetings for the next two weeks, You're going to have to get my flights cancelled.'

The following day the pilot went to his Commissar and asked for the next two weeks off, and received the predictable, negative reply. He wondered if it was an accident when in the post the following day he received a demand that he serve on a jury for the next fifteen days. That gave him the opportunity to attend the Christian meetings held in the evenings.

Steeped in atheism but just a little curious about Christ, the pilot turned up at the second Christian meeting. That time Zachary prayed for rain. It was the summer of 1991. The steppes of Russia were parched dry and if, as seemed likely, the harvest failed, there would be famine in the already-anarchic country the following winter.

When the pilot heard Zachary pray for rain he said to himself, 'Got you! You obviously don't understand the climate of this country. It doesn't change like that. I know what the barometer reading is. I know the direction from which the wind is blowing. Rain is absolutely, physically impossible.'

That night there was a rain storm over hundreds of square miles of the Russian Republic.

When we've worked out our systematic theologies, pushed God in a box or, for preference, written Him out of the script completely — atheistic General Lawrence Fuller is cured of cancer, Jen Larcombe stomps up the steps with her wheelchair in tow and God makes it rain on Russia.

Such miracles point to the future. They are appetizers

of a heavenly feast to come. They are insights into God's ideal world, of paradise restored when sin and its author have been removed.

This is the promise of Job 42. Wrongs will be righted. And those who, like Job's children, have died in disaster will rise in resurrection to live eternally.

---

[1] Peter Masters, *The Healing Epidemic* (Wakeman, London, 1988).
[2] Job 42:3, NIV.
[3] Job 19:23-26, NIV.
[4] Job 38:1; 40:6.
[5] Mark 9:35-37; 10:14, 15.

17 When miracles don't happen

Meanwhile, back at the ranch . . . in this imperfect world in which 10-year-old Samantha has leukaemia, and they've just told me that Mike — cured of cancer twice — has a malignant growth in his bowel, and that the morbid retention of fluid that has caused the swelling may suggest a problem in the kidneys . . . and in which Marion is having a bad day with her MS . . .

. . . in this tear-washed world in which we live and move . . . the biggest thing that bugs the Christian sick is often guilt that they *are* sick induced by Job's comforters who are saying that their healing is blocked by lack of faith . . . . Jen Larcombe heard that so many times from visitors in the early days of her disorder that she thought of banning visitors!

Rex Gardner, now a consultant paediatrician, then a humble GP, once wrote this on a patient's notes when referring her to a psychiatrist: 'Part of this woman's problem is her conviction that as a Christian she should not be ill. Therefore, she is in a cleft stick: either God is letting her down, or she is letting God down.'[1] Either way, she couldn't handle it and had developed a psychiatric disorder.

Twenty-one detailed case-studies are contained in Kathryn Kuhlman's book. At the conclusion of the book she poses the question: 'Why are some healed and others not?'[2] She ponders the issue of faith. What is it? Is it something that you can manufacture? Or work up? Or receive as a reward for good works?

If there are such things as 'key texts', the 'key text' about faith has to be, 'By grace you have been saved, through faith — and this not from yourselves, it is the gift of God — not by works, so that no one can boast.'[3] Here

Paul is dealing with faith as it relates to salvation. But faith is the same substance when it relates to healing. And faith, apparently, cannot be worked up or merited — because it is a gift. Faith, a gift. Salvation, a gift. Healing, a gift. Gifts of God's grace: salvation a gift given to those who want it, healing a gift *not* given on demand.

After a life-time of teaching and preaching about healing, Kathryn Kuhlman concluded that tremendous psychological damage was inflicted by those standing on the spiritual high ground, and hollering 'Lack of faith!' at anyone who, in any one of a score of different ways, had asked for healing and not received it. She found that those involved in full-time, stage-managed healing ministries were particularly prone to invoke the 'lack of faith' accusation when someone was unhealed. It seemed both to explain God's inaction and, more importantly, let the healer off the hook! She described instances in which she herself had felt 'crushed': on the one hand there was a God of limitless power; on the other there were sick who were unhealed.[4]

There's quite a spectrum of responses to the 'Wot-no-miracles?' question. At one end are those who expect nothing and receive nothing because their theology allows no place for miracles today — or, perhaps, at any other period. At the other end is the miracle-a-minute brigade who lay hands on anyone, anywhere, any time, and declare them healed.

The response of those who profess not to believe in healing is similar to that of the would-be atheist who can't quite make it to 100 per cent unbelief in God: There's no meaning, no significance to anything; everything is random — but they're irritated with God when He doesn't heal anyway!

Those who regard illness as a sign of spiritual weakness and demand healing as a right — and attribute the absence of healing to lack of faith — dredge through the New

Testament and manage to throw up one text. Jesus did very few miracles in His home town 'because of their lack of faith'.[5] They overlook the many instances in which the faith or lack of faith of the individual is not even mentioned, and in which healing is given before the matter of sin is dealt with.[6]

The fact is, of course, that both the 'healing never' and the 'healing ever' positions are at variance with Scripture.[7] Foraging through the Bible for a foundation for their belief the scholars of the extremes have come up with mutually incompatible conclusions. The exegesis of one group suggests that the gifts of the Spirit were 'inaugural', hence restricted to the early part of the Acts; despite abundant evidence of the use of the Spirit's gifts today. The biblical exegesis of the other group suggests that physical healing is granted to anyone with enough faith; despite abundant evidence that it doesn't work like that.

Most of the books available on the subject of healing appear to be arguing one or other of these extreme positions. The result? Confusion and frustration.

Having come up in the 'healing ever' school, Kathryn Kuhlman was almost broken as she beheld 'the looks of despair and disappointment' on the faces of those slinking away from a big tent divine healing service unhealed. The sight had haunted her for weeks; 'Was this, then, the God of all mercy and great compassion? I remember that night how, with tears streaming down my face, I looked up and cried: "They have taken away my Lord and I know not where they have laid Him", and I remember going to my room and sobbing out my heart to God, praying for light on the truth.'[8]

From his experience with divine healing, and as a physician and surgeon, Rex Gardner has a message for the 'healing never' and 'healing ever' schools of theology: 'When you're comparing scripture with scripture — glance out of the window from time to time! See what God is doing in today's world!'[9]

The fact is, of course, that *any* attempt by *any* group of theologians to saddle the Great Physician with *any* structure of rules and regulations within which He must operate will end up with egg on their faces. If they will 'glance out of the window' they will find God doing all kinds of amazing things in this materialistic age. Taking people by surprise, taking the unexpected route, just as He always has done.

That was how it was with Jesus. The received theological wisdom of the first century pronounced it impossible that a blind man could receive his sight given certain circumstances. The finest scholars available presented their arguments to the blind man, and he listened. Then he said: 'I only know one thing. Once I was blind, now I see.'[10]

One erstwhile blind man who could see. That was the evidence 'out of the window', theological argumentation notwithstanding.

Kuhlman received an answer when she prayed for 'light on the truth' about healing and faith. To her surprise, a 'very fine Christian lady' interrupted her sermon one evening. She felt that the Holy Spirit had prompted her. Kuhlman's conclusion from the words of the interrupter? 'The Holy Spirit, then, was the answer: an answer so profound that no human being can fathom the full extent of its depth and power, and yet so simple that most folk miss it!'[11] In short, there was no set procedure for healing. No need for 'wild exhortations to have faith' or 'healing virtue', for 'the Spirit blows wherever it pleases'.[12]

After years of ministry, Kuhlman reached the conclusion that faith was not a 'quality or power by which the things desired become the things possessed'. Faith was not a substance to be quantified or confined in a container. It was a gift of God's grace. And the wonder of it all was that the gift was often given when the recipient felt least deserving. 'The faith imparted to the sinner for salvation is solely the result of God's mercy and grace. It is a gift. The faith that is imparted to the individual for the healing of his physical body is again only the result of God's mercy; the overflow of His great compassion and grace. It is a gift. You do not pray for faith; you seek the Lord, and faith will come.' Faith was in the presence of the Master — and being aware of it. [13]

Physician-surgeon Rex Gardner, after examining scores of miracle case histories, reached the same conclusion but added one word of caution: 'Not all miracles come from God; they can be satanic, occultic.' Elsewhere he warns against undue credulousness with regard to healing stories past and present. [14] Similarly, throughout his career, Dr. Martyn Lloyd-Jones gave this kind of warning: 'We must still continue to maintain our healthy, sceptical and critical attitude to everything that is reported to us.' In the Olivet sermon of Jesus, in Paul's apocalyptic passage in the second letter to the Thessalonians and in the book of Revelation warnings are given that the end-time world will witness diabolic miracles. [15] The New Age movement's preoccupation with various forms of occultic healing techniques may be seen as a partial fulfilment of these prophecies. [16]

While, as in the case of General Lawrence Fuller, God may perform a miracle prior to prayer, this is exceptional. Miraculous healings in the Christian Church take place after prayer in the name of Jesus. [17]

Whether a given healing is deemed 'miraculous' depends on our definition of 'miracle'. C. S. Lewis: 'An interference with nature by supernatural power.' James Packer: 'A particular kind of physical event having spiritual significance and value.' Rex Gardner: 'The healing of organic disease by means, or at a speed, inexplicable medically and preceded by prayer in the name of Jesus Christ.'

There are endless discussions of definitions as well as classifications of 'types' of miracles.[18] The most exhaustive is found in C. S. Lewis's book, *Miracles*. Everything, Lewis argues, depends on our presuppositions; our objectivity is governed by our subjectivity. He argues that, even if the end of the world occurred as described in Scripture — the ubiquitous appearance of Jesus in the skies 'as the lightning dazzles from east to west' — the modern materialist would merely regard it as an illusion and find an explanation in terms of psychoanalysis or cerebral pathology.

If our presuppositions include a belief in an all-powerful and all-loving God, then miracles are not a problem. When Jesus turned the water into wine it would be a case of a God who, year by year, turns water into wine through vines, short-circuiting His own process by making wine in a moment.[19] Similarly with healing. The God who would, at the resurrection, change our 'vile body, that it may be fashioned like unto his glorious body',[20] merely chooses to do His renewing work locally and temporarily through healing.

Such miracles of healing are not done in the interests of sensationalism, but as a tiny glimpse into what He will one day do on a far grander scale — and to provide proof of His love and concern.

Guilt trips laid on unhealed Christians: lack-of-faith or sin-in-the-life.

Guilt trips laid on *healed* Christians: Why you? Why not everybody?

Part of Jen Larcombe's defence against the second type of guilt trip is to argue that her dramatic healing was *not* a miracle. She has been interviewed repeatedly on TV and by the press and every interviewer has asked: 'If God has the power to heal you, why not put the whole world to rights?' When I interviewed her we spent some time discussing the question, 'Is God unfair?' Jen feels that Paul is discussing this question in Romans 9 and that he reaches his conclusion when he cites the words of God to Moses; ' "I will have mercy on whom I have mercy, and I will have compassion on whom I have compassion." '[21] Paul was discussing salvation, but what he says applies also to healing; when I show mercy, it's pure mercy — human effort does not contribute to it. With patience, love and compassion God says: 'My thoughts are not your thoughts, and your ways are not my ways . . . . For as the heavens are higher than the earth, so are my ways higher than your ways and my thoughts than your thoughts.'[22]

But our restless minds need to reason further. This may be part of the answer to the 'Is God unfair?' question. We live on a planet in rebellion; mankind has declared UDI. Not only have we declared unilaterally our independence of God — we flaunt that independence. This is why God is not free to act for our good in all things. But He is working to reverse the rebellion. Calvary is the key. It makes possible reconciliation between God and man, subject to man's choice. An eternal kingdom is coming in which there will be no sickness and hence no need for healing. The healing miracles we see today are like snowdrops, the front runners of spring. And the coming of springtime is as certain as the promises of God.

Meanwhile, what help does God provide for the unhealed?

---

[1] Rex Gardner, *A Doctor Investigates Healing Miracles* (Darton, Longman and Todd, 1986), page 1.

[2] Kathryn Kuhlman, *I Believe in Miracles: God's Power to Heal Today* (Marshall, Pickering, 1963), page 196.

[3] Ephesians 2:8, 9, NIV.

[4] Kuhlman, op cit.

[5] Matthew 13:53-58, NIV.

[6] eg Matthew 12:9-14; John 5:1-15.

[7] Michael Poole, *Miracles, Science, the Bible and Experience* (Scripture Union, 1992), pages 103-113.

[8] Kuhlman, op cit, page 197.

[9] Gardner, op cit, page 5.

[10] John 9.

[11] Kuhlman, op cit, pages 198-200.

[12] John 3:8, NIV.

[13] Kuhlman, op cit, page 203.

[14] Gardner, pages 7 and 6-17.

[15] Matthew 24:4, 5, 11, 23-26; 2 Thessalonians 2:5-12; Revelation 13:13; 16:12-15.

[16] See David Marshall, *New Age Versus the Gospel* (Autumn House, 1993).

[17] Romans 10:9; 1 John 4:2, 3; James 5:14, 15.

[18] Poole, op cit, pages 102-113; Gardner, op cit, pages, 1, 12; C. S. Lewis, *Miracles* (Collins, 1947), page 9.

[19] John 2:1-10.

[20] Philippians 3:21.

[21] Romans 9:14, 15, NIV.

[22] Isaiah 55:8, 9, NEB.

18 Hope for the unhealed

The legion of the bereaved, the suffering and the starving
. . . the fellowship of the fearful, the wretched of the earth,
those in pain, sporadic or pandemic . . . the victims of mal-
nutrition or of the well-nourished who wage wars . . . .

For them there is no reasoning-things-through, no adequate theology they can believe or, perhaps, even bear to
listen to, not now . . . the mother whose teenage son has
just committed suicide, the proud dad who has just seen
his 3-year-old 'Tiger' hit dead by a drunken driver . . . .

'The God of all comfort . . . comforts us in all our
troubles, so that we can comfort those in any trouble with
the comfort we ourselves have received from God.' So we
are His arms, His feet, His voice in a pain-wretched world.
'For just as the sufferings of Christ flow into our lives, so
also through Christ our comfort overflows.'[1]

But *does* it though? Or are we stuck for words to say,
even thoughts to think . . . for the instant, the world unin-
telligible, the mystery over-mastering?

I have found that when other helpers fail, and it seems
to be down to me, and the sufferer appears comfortless —
words are, in any event, redundant. The need is not so
much for answers — there *are* no glib one-liners to cover
these situations — but for a loving arm around the
shoulders, someone to weep with the weeper, to listen to
every outpouring of words and never repeat them. The elo-
quence of empathetic silence is very often the Jesus way.
And when the Spirit prompts there will be an opportunity
for prayer, maybe silent, maybe shared.

Away from crisis situations, what's to be said to those to
whom pain and, perhaps, indignity are constant companions?

Before you say a word, allow for the fact that they know a lot more about it all than you do. There are some tough cookies in this class. You see, God doesn't *always* wait for your hands, feet and voice box to get active in His behalf. He hurts with the hurting and, when we are sluggish, gets active in the situation in Person. 'Suffering colours life,' observed the pious to the pained. 'Yes,' said the pained, 'but I choose the colour.' God had dropped in already. Often does. I've known MS sufferers and cancer cases to have enough trust/strength of character/fidelity (choose your own word; God gave it) to be humorists and incurably optimistic — *most* of the time.

In some cases the only work God may have left you to do is dig the garden, get the TV repair man in and do a spot of shopping.

Before you start into theologizing, remember: Unless you have, don't talk as if you've been there. If you have been there, your words are of much greater value. This is why Jen Larcombe's life is so full: phone calls, consultations, meetings. She's been there and God has made her well to minister to those who are still there. J. M. Barrie's mother lost a son; 'That was where she got her soft eyes from,' Barrie said, 'and why other mothers ran to her when they lost a child.' It was said of Jesus Himself, 'Because He Himself had gone through it, He is able to help others who are going through it.'[2]

John Newton, slave trader turned Christian minister, learned a lot of lessons about suffering, helping the sufferers and surviving with his own sanity intact. For long months he was obliged to watch his wife die a lingering, painful death from cancer. He reached a point where, identifying with his wife's distress, he was almost destroyed; 'I believe it was about two or three months before her death,' he wrote, 'when I was walking up and down the room, offering disjointed prayers from a heart torn with distress, that a thought suddenly struck me with unusual force to this effect — "The promises of God must be true; surely the Lord will help me, *if I am willing to be helped!*" ' He discovered that his personal willingness to be helped proved the secret, not only of his own survival, but of bringing peace and solace to the final weeks of his wife's existence. The Holy Spirit led him through Scripture to find power enough for two.[3]

We should never lose sight of the fact that healing is, in the strictest sense, holistic: body, mind, spirit:

☐ Spiritual healing is fundamental because it means our salvation and has an eternal dimension.

☐ God can bring the healing of the mind, even in the midst of the worst of pain; Jesus offers indestructible peace beyond the understanding of the materialist to all who ask Him. And promises that, in the ultimate, the world need hold no terrors because He has fought them and beaten them.[4] And, as always, the peace that Jesus offers is *shalom*; not merely the absence of trouble, but the conviction that the limitless power of the Almighty — despite every appearance to the contrary — is working out our highest good.

☐ It is, of course, entirely natural that those in pain should reach out for *physical* healing. At times, however, as with Jen Larcombe, the peace-joy comes only when we stop badgering God, and rest content that He has our best good at heart. One local pastor had a brain tumour. His whole congregation prayed for his healing. It seemed as if one church member, in her daily devotions, received each day some spiritual insight that would help her pastor. She would write it down and push it through his letter-box. One day she received the insight: *'I will heal him in My nearer presence.'* Though she wrote the thought down, she was shattered and dared not pass the message on to her pastor. This is the hardest message to bear. The answer to the question 'Will He heal us here?' is simply this: We cannot know, but we are entitled, indeed we are *invited*, to ask Him.

For many years I refused to add the phrase 'If it be Thy will' to any prayer for healing. To me it seemed both an evidence of lack of faith (a let-out for God) and a blasphemy. I felt that I *knew* that it was *always* God's will to bring healing. Now I realize that my refusal to employ this rider to my prayers implied a presumptuous belief in everyone's entitlement to physical health — *right then*. 'If it be Thy will' is to place the sufferer in the safest pair of hands possible; we need to leave more, not less, to God in our prayers.

Physician-surgeon Rex Gardner spent a life-time researching case histories of healing. He thought it plausible to put at least 600 claimed cancer cures down to 'spontaneous remission'.[5] But he found many more case histories in which 'spontaneous remission' emphatically was *not* the explanation for the cancer cure. Nor was 'incorrect diagnosis', 'therapeutic response' or any 'psychosomatic-type' explanation. He details many instances in which 'spontaneous *resolution*' — through the preserving intercession of God — was the answer, not 'spontaneous *remission*'.[6]

It is Gardner's emphatic conviction that miracles did not end with Acts but 'have continued throughout the Christian age'. Miracles were not, he asserts, a sort of 'first-stage rocket' designed to fall away from the Church when it was safely in orbit.[7] The evidence of Scripture is that the power of the Holy Spirit will be available to the Church until the end of time.

Is it possible that the 'strange-goings-on' congregations have made mainstream Christianity altogether too cautious about the role of the Holy Spirit? Can it be that the undeniable evidence that there *is* a counterfeit has made us deny the real, to cut the Holy Spirit out completely? If this is the case, are the sick waiting on a revived Church for healing? A Church less inward-looking? A Church whose members do not jabber unintelligibly to one another either in tongues or in religious jargon words and phrases? A Church that is, in short, open to the Holy Spirit?

Revivalist David Watson believed that to be the case. On film he sought to illustrate the impact of the Holy Spirit in latter-rain outpouring on the staid and tidy ways of the Church. His office desk was neat and tidy, piles of papers carefully placed in significant positions. Then he flung open the window and let in the wind. The tidy pattern disappeared in a swirl of papers. In Greek, the same word serves for both *Spirit* and *wind*. And the evidence of Scripture is that the wind of the Holy Spirit is not the 'gentle zephyr' of the hymn, but a 'violent' or 'driving' wind.[8]

Is it possible that when the windows of the church are fully open to the Holy Spirit a great deal of the present practice of the Church right across the theological spectrum will be blown about? That the Spirit will pay less attention to denominational allegiance than we do? That miraculous healings will suddenly be in much greater evidence? That was certainly the belief that filled the preaching and gripped the life of Dr. Martyn Lloyd-Jones in the last decade of his fruitful ministry.[9]

Michael Poole in *Miracles: Science, the Bible and Experience* reached that conclusion. As the kingdom draws near, he said, the Holy Spirit will be more and more evident in the Church, making Christ and His Gospel known, and in miraculous works, including healing. He says, 'Perhaps one reason for the dearth of miracles is the rather sickly state of the Church in many places . . . .'[10]

John White in *When the Spirit Comes With Power* is undeniably influenced by both Martyn Lloyd-Jones and David Watson. He is impatient for the coming of the Spirit. Impatient with the conservatism of the Church. Wanting to open both doors and windows to the 'rushing mighty wind' that will, again, make miracles a frequent part of the

Church's outreach. He insists that every Spirit-influenced revival has had both a human and a divine side. The 'strange doings' aspect of revivals, he says, is no more than the manifestation of the human side. The Spirit's power will always be exercised to positive, definite purpose.[11]

There is a growing feeling in most wings of the Church that the last phase in the Church's history will be like the first phase.

When Jesus *ascended* to the throne at His Father's right hand, the Spirit *descended* to His throne. And the throne of the Spirit is the Church. When the Spirit came, the disciples — who had run from Gethsemane, been despondent, divided, disillusioned or simply absent at Calvary, and, even after the resurrection, had had to be chided for their unwillingness to believe — were transformed. Suddenly there was a holy boldness — *and* an outbreak of miracles. Quite a transformation! Is there anyone who believes that the Church cannot use such a transformation now?

In urgent words on the night of His betrayal, Jesus had told the disciples of the imminent arrival of the Spirit. Told them that the purpose of the Spirit's arrival would be to 'testify of me'. Had emphasized 'for he shall not speak of himself'.[12] Hence those truly 'baptized by the Spirit' will not constantly be talking about the Spirit, or be speaking about their experience in the Spirit, but will be preaching the good news about the Lord Jesus Christ.

On the day of Pentecost, the Spirit-transformed Peter, at the conclusion of his sermon to the Sanhedrin, indicated that the power of the Holy Spirit was available to all who accepted the name of Jesus and were covered by His righteousness.[13] Is there a gift which is ours by right but not ours by possession? Have we been satisfied with half-filled cups when the river of God might be flowing through our lives? Is the Church preventing the Holy Spirit from doing all He would like to do in the area of healing?

Two final words of comfort to the suffering.

First, you are in good company. You are part of the great 'fellowship of Christ's sufferings'.[14] While suffering has a levelling effect among believers — afflicting rich and poor, powerful and weak, schooled and unschooled — it encompassed Jesus; to Paul, pain was a privilege because, in some measure, it meant sharing in the sufferings of Christ. It was part of the refinement of character that brought out the image of Jesus in human life. Paul had lived his life with 'a bodily ailment, a sharp rankling pain' which God had declined to take away, despite Paul's repeated requests. But God had given him the assurance He gives to all sufferers: ' "My grace is sufficient for you." '[15]

Second, the great day is coming when disease, suffering and death will be done away with for ever.

Every miraculous healing points to that day. And few healings can have been more dramatically miraculous or as well witnessed and documented as that of Roy Slaybaugh . . . .

[1] 2 Corinthians 1:3-7, NIV.

[2] William Barclay's paraphrase of Hebrews 2:18 in *The Letters to the Corinthians* (St. Andrews, 1954), page 191.

[3] Cited, Jerry Bridges, *Trusting God Even When Life Hurts* (Scripture Press, 1989), page 195.

[4] John 14:27; John 16:33. See also 14:1-3.

[5] K. M. Hay, 'Survival Against the Odds', *British Medical Journal*, 291 (1985), pages 1085-1086; T. C. Everson and W. H. Cole, 'Spontaneous Regression of Cancer: Preliminary Report', *Annals of Surgery*, 144 (1956), pages 366-383.

[6] Rex Gardner, *A Doctor Investigates Healing Miracles*, op cit, pages 25-41, 199, *et seq*.

[7] Ibid, page 130.

[8] Acts 2:2, NIV and NEB.

[9] See D. Martyn Lloyd-Jones, *Joy Unspeakable* (Kingsway, 1984).

[10] Michael Poole, op cit, pages 103-113. See especially page 109.

[11] John White, *When the Spirit Comes With Power* (Hodder, Revised Edition, 1992), pages 169, 173.

[12] John 15:26; 16:13, 14.

[13] Acts 2:38, 39.

[14] Philippians 3:10.

[15] 2 Corinthians 12:7-9, NIV; Philippians 3:8-10; Gardner, op cit, pages 188-191, Bridges, op cit, pages 189-191.

19 One chance in a million

The surgeon at Gold Beach Hospital, Oregon, was nothing if not frank.

He told Rose Slaybaugh that Roy's prospect of recovery was 'one chance in a million'.

It was Sunday 19 August 1945, and the flower of American surgical know-how, along with the flower of American youth, was still overseas embroiled in the death-throes of World War II.

Hence, when the accident happened, the Gold Beach Hospital, Oregon, was mainly staffed by retired surgeons and physicians.

It was strange how, that morning, Roy had seemed reluctant to leave home. Though not given to premonitions, after family worship he had insisted on saying a second prayer for God's watch-care that day. Before he left the house, he made Rose promise not to leave it. To him, the danger in the air was so real as to be almost tangible.

But as it happened, it was Roy who was in danger. Not Rose.

That morning two boys had broken out of the Oregon State Penitentiary. There was a degree of pre-planning; guns and a car were at their disposal. Police in pursuit, they headed south at kamikaze speed.

The first car was dumped. They picked up another. But the police, sirens blaring, were soon on their trail.

The chase was along the coast highway, in those days a winding stretch of road with sharp bends, and a deep ravine on one side where it was dangerous to exceed 30mph. In their stolen car the boys were travelling at between 85 and 90mph.

It was just after 9am when they hit Roy Slaybaugh's car. The impact was such that the cars, 'just doubled around one another', became inextricable. The police had never seen a worse accident with lower chances of survival.

But the youthful criminals *did* survive.

With Roy, it was a different story.

The news of the accident was brought to Rose by Pastor Fred Wimer around one o'clock. His wife Vicky was especially comforting. At that stage they merely conveyed the idea that Roy was hurt and in hospital. 'Is he badly hurt?' Rose wanted to know. There were long faces and no answers.

The surgeon was with Roy when Rose entered Intensive Care. The impact had been to Roy's head which was almost completely covered with bandages. At the foot of the bed were his blood-soaked clothes and shoes which, through a terrible oversight, had not been removed.

Rose: 'Doctor, please tell me, how badly is my husband hurt?'

Doctor: 'Very badly.'

'I can see that. But I mean, what are his chances for life?'

Doctor: 'Mrs. Slaybaugh, you're asking me a very frank question.'

'Doctor, I must have a frank answer. There are only the two of us. There are certain things to be thought of and planned.'

Doctor: 'Of course, you should know. I can't give you very much hope for his recovery. Perhaps one chance in a million .... He has a compound fracture of the skull, and the cerebral fluid is draining out of the left eye and ear. There is no possible way of stopping it.'

'Then I must hurry and send for his people,' said Rose.

The surgeon wanted to know where they would be coming from. When he was told Portland and Seattle he said there would be no point in sending for them; it would be a wasted journey.

Thus began Rose's vigil by the bedside, shared by a succession of nurses. 'Please,' Rose begged, 'don't ask me to leave his bedside until it's all over.'

Two doctors and two nurses were present as the bandages were removed from Roy's head. Rose was permitted to stay. A severed ear had been tucked up in the bandage. Rose made for the fresh air. A nurse caught up with her to reassure her that the ear could be 'sewn back on'.

The surgeons and doctors were examining X-ray pictures showing a fractured skull and broken jawbones. It was then twenty-four hours since the accident and the cerebral fluid was still oozing out of the eye and ear.

The ear *was* sewn back on. 'If he lives,' reassured the surgeon, 'we can get an artificial ear made for him.'

Of greater concern was Roy's eye; 'Mrs. Slaybaugh, the sight of the left eye is destroyed.' Rose had been prepared for that; no left eye had been visible when the bandages had been removed. Again there was the reassurance that, in the event of Roy's survival, an artificial eye could be made for him.

When Rose asked the question, 'What about his mind?' she received no answer.

During the second night's vigil by Roy's bedside, Rose was given permission to telephone relations. Soon relatives on both sides of the family were on their way.

On Tuesday afternoon death was close. The membranes of Roy's throat had collapsed. He had never regained consciousness. He was gasping for breath. His tongue had swollen to an unbelievable extent. It had been severely injured when he had been thrown over the steering wheel and through the windscreen.

Again there was an urgent little consultation with the doctors. They told Rose how critically ill Roy was and how there was little hope for his recovery. Already the relatives had worked that out for themselves. In the hallway Rose overheard the words, 'As soon as it's all over, I'll drive you home in my car so you can get your family in your car and be back in time for the funeral.' Rose heard Vicky Wimer say, 'As soon as it's over, we're going to take Rose back home with us in our car.'

Detailed plans were being made for the funeral. The body would be taken to their home town Spokane by rail. Someone was dispatched to the Slaybaugh home to pick up Roy's dark suit and new white shirt.

But Rose noticed that something was preoccupying Pastor Wimer. He drew her aside and asked her if she had thought of calling together ministers to anoint Roy. Punch-drunk from lack of sleep, Rose did not understand. At four o'clock on Wednesday morning Wimer urged this course of action, quoting James 5:14, 15; 'Is any sick among you? Let him call for the elders of the church; and let them pray over him, anointing him with oil in the name of the Lord: and the prayer of faith shall save the sick, and the Lord shall raise him up; and if he has committed sins, they shall be forgiven him.'

It was not until some hours later that the importance of this course of action recommended itself to Rose's mind. 'Hurry, hurry, and do it!' she said. 'Roy is dying! We don't have very much time left.'

Wimer wanted another minister with him when the anointing service took place. Rose suggested her old pastor from Portland. Portland, however, was ten hours away. She settled for Pastor T. L. Thuemler of Crescent City. A phone call was made. He was soon on the way.

'At ten minutes to twelve', Rose has written, 'the doctor stepped in on his way home for lunch. He picked up Roy's hands, looked at the darkened nails, and tenderly laid them down. Then he reached across the bed and patted me on the shoulder, and without a word he went out.'

At noon the anointing service took place. The ministers closed the door. Those present were Pastor Thuemler who was to do the anointing, Pastor and Mrs. Wimer, Rose's brother, Roy's brother Joe, his two sons, the wife of one of the sons, and Rose.

At first they stood around Roy's bed. 'Are there any unbelievers in this room?' Pastor Thuemler asked. 'If so, would you please leave.' Rose glanced at her two nephews. She knew that those six-foot tall young men had no religious convictions. But they did not leave.

The pastor invited everyone to kneel. Everyone did, except Rose. She took Roy's two hands and held them up as if to God.

Pastor Wimer prayed a moving prayer. Pastor Thuemler pleaded with God to spare Roy's life and anointed him in the name of the Father, the Son and the Holy Spirit, pouring oil over his hand and reaching up to touch the tiny part of Roy's head that was not bandaged.

The second Thuemler's hand touched Roy's forehead, a shudder passed through the previously inert frame of the patient. The pastor continued his prayer. Rose continued to hold Roy's hands but, on opening her eyes, noticed that Roy had closed his mouth over his swollen tongue and was breathing through his nose normally. The swellings around his face and jaw appeared to recede. A nose seemed to take shape, then a mouth, then a chin, and it was clear that the throat-swelling was disappearing.

Everyone stood, weeping. Pastor Thuemler said, 'We'll all go out quietly. Roy is going to be all right.' He reached down and took one of Roy's hands. Roy gripped it tight. Subsequently, Thuemler said, 'I'll never forget that handshake as long as I live.'

As he headed for the door, Rose pleaded, 'Please, not yet.' The nurses came in and were staggered by the change in Roy. The man with two broken jaws was yawning!

The doctor entered. Unaware of what had happened, he looked at the patient in disbelief. Even Roy's fingernails were the natural colour. The doctor removed the bandage from Roy's left eye. Rose had watched him change the dressing on the eye cavity from day to day. No eye had been visible. *But there was an eye!* The doctor passed his hand quickly over it, back and forth, and exclaimed: 'And there's sight in it!'

Before leaving the room somewhat unnerved, the doctor exclaimed: 'This man's going to live! And more than that, he's got an eye with sight in it!'

Roy was conscious then. After a few 'Hellos' he said he was famished. Not surprising; it was Wednesday afternoon and he hadn't eaten since Sunday.

Roy asked about the accident. After hearing the description he wanted to know; 'Was anyone hurt?'

'Yes, you're smashed all to pieces,' Rose answered.

'Oh,' Roy said, 'I don't feel anything. I don't feel a thing.'

There had been not one moment of pain from all those injuries. Scars remained on Roy's forehead. They were unprepared for the sight when the bandages were removed from his ear; 'That's a beautiful ear!' exclaimed the nurse. Roy expressed amusement at that; ears, he said, were never beautiful! Not even his!

One week after the accident, Roy Slaybaugh walked out of the hospital. Behind him were nurses, doctors and surgeons who were obliged to believe the evidence of their senses and have committed their signed statements to paper.

Roy's jaws did not have to be wired or set. There was no need for an artificial ear or eye. The anticipated surgery on Roy's tongue never needed to be done.

Perhaps the left eye was the most surprising aspect of all. When the insurance had been sorted out and a replacement car acquired, it was necessary for Roy to retake his driving test. That he did without difficulty, but he wondered what would happen when the test official said, 'Now we'll see how your eyes are, Mr. Slaybaugh. How far down the card can you read these letters?'

Roy: 'I can read the bottom line if you want.'

The official thought Roy had possibly memorized the letters and said, 'We'll turn the card over. Now, how far down can you read?'

Roy read the bottom line, backwards and forwards.

'You have remarkable sight for a man of your age,' said the official. 'What can you do with one eye?' He picked up an envelope and covered one eye.

Roy could still read the bottom line backwards and forwards.

'You have the eyes of an eagle!'

At home later Roy expressed relief; 'Rose, it was a good thing he covered up my old eye, or I couldn't even have seen the cardboard!'

The repercussions of Roy's healing were tremendous. All those concerned committed their testimonies to paper and signed them. They were published in the book *Escape From Death* (Southern Publishing Association, Nashville, Tennessee, 1953). Many came to Christ, including the two 'unbelieving' nephews, and a number of nurses. Perhaps, most remarkably, the two young criminals came to Christ.

Knowing he had been healed by the direct intervention of the Great Physician, Roy Slaybaugh decided to visit the two boys, back in the penitentiary. He told his story. And, over the weeks, introduced them to the Gospel. Their hearts were changed. They came to Christ. On their release they enrolled in ministerial training. Twenty years after Roy's healing, men and women were still being brought to Christ as a result of it.

Dr. Peter Masters has written; 'James 5, written as early as AD 45-50, stands alone as the directive to Christians who do not possess the rare, first-century gifts referred to by Paul as the signs of an apostle.'[1] Certainly in the case of Roy Slaybaugh, 'the elders of the church' had been called together, and 'the prayer of faith had saved the sick'.

Of the scores of testimonies that impinged upon the healing of Roy Slaybaugh, Roy's own testimony is the most remarkable:

'I would like to add my testimony and tell you what I experienced during the time of my healing. I will try to give an exact account of it.

'There appeared at the foot of my bed a heavenly being, beautiful beyond description. It was head and shoulders taller than an ordinary man. I say 'man' because he was masculine-looking. His hair was light gold in colour and hung in ringlets about his head. He was clothed in a beautiful white robe which hung in pleats around his shoulders to the floor and gathered at the waist by a golden girdle with tassels hanging down his right side.

'He gave me a very reassuring look, but I hardly dared look at him. He said, "I have come to raise you up again." And with that he reached over and touched me. It must have been just as the minister anointed me, for a great fear and trembling came over me, and I became fully conscious. He looked the same as he did in my semi-conscious state, but he was so glorious I had to take my gaze away from him.

'I looked about the room and wondered where I was and why all these people, our friends and relatives, were there, and why they were weeping, but my mind was on this beautiful being at the foot of the bed. I was almost afraid to look back, and when I did, he had disappeared. He must have known that I couldn't take another look and live. If this being is an indication of what heaven will be like, or what we will be when we have put on immortality and have been changed "in a moment, in the twinkling of an eye, at the last trump" (1 Corinthians 15:52), heaven will be cheap at any price.'[2]

[1] Peter Masters, *The Healing Epidemic* (Wakeman, London, 1988), page 136.
[2] Rose Slaybaugh, *Escape From Death* (Southern Publishing Association, Nashville, Tennessee, 1953), page 106.

20 A great expectation

While high theologians debate questions like 'Can we believe in miracles in a scientific age?' God smiles broadly at the impertinent use to which they put the fragment of information they have managed to nail down. And He gets on with the job.

Roy Slaybaugh mends miraculously after being the victim of motoring mayhem. General Fuller is healed by a God whose existence he has denied. After eight years in a wheelchair, Jen Larcombe, after a simple prayer, walks tall, then runs into high-level health. And a thousand-and-one ordinary people praise God from whom all blessings flow as He raises them up, makes them whole, puts death, disease and disaster into reverse in ways major and minor — all through the power of prayer.

But paeans of praise are cried down by the howls of the hurting on this not-so-silent planet. And then there is the anguish of those who die quietly because they are too hungry to stay alive; and the soft sobs of the little children, bleeding from shrapnel wounds from the crossfire of a hundred wars fought for reasons long forgotten, or from the bullets of terrorists whose arcane causes they will not grow up to understand, the technical term for whose particular psychopathic disorder they will never be old enough to pronounce.

For the world wails in travail. Man is sick. And God is no longer smiling indulgently. He hurts with the hurting, agonizes with those who agonize, falls with the fallen and longs to draw the line: *Enough!*

Direct intervention at Bethlehem, the healings in the cities of Galilee and Judaea and the reconciling death on Calvary made inevitable a second, final, far-more-dramatic

intervention. Evil, death, disease and the devil were con-
clusively beaten at the battle outside Jerusalem's walls in
AD 31. But their outworking continues to manifest itself in
ever-more-gigantic   disasters: megafamines,   megafloods,
megadeath. All symptoms of a planet in its death throes. Indicators that God is going to call closing-time.

Physical, mental and spiritual wholeness will be experienced only in God's kingdom. The trees whose leaves are
for the healing of the nations[1] do not grow around here.
Here is present imperfect. Here is famine, bacteria and
trauma — until Time becomes Eternity.

Tomorrow is God's, and in that tomorrow pain, sorrow,
famine and injustice will only be distant memories, if that.
Miracles in present imperfect are but tiny windows through
which the eternal purpose of God shines out into a world at
midnight. God's present economy of miracles demonstrates
that He *is* still in the healing business. The gifts of God to
the Church at its inception[2] indicate that, through a revived
Church, He could heal — and not just physically — far
more effectively, act far more frequently . . . for we are His
hands and feet and voice . . . .

But God's greatest work of healing will happen in the
future, in His nearer presence, after a second dramatic intervention in the planet's affairs.

Facing a sunset-framed temple in the week before Calvary, Jesus prophesied Jerusalem's fall and His own return
in glory. He detailed the indicators that would herald His
arrival. Described the manner of that arrival, the challenge
of that arrival and the purpose of that arrival. And the substance of His message has been the Church's great expec-
tation.[3] To assume that Matthew, Mark, Luke — and Jesus
— were confused, if not mistaken, regarding the fall of Jerusalem and the Return is not an option. The whole of

Scripture rustles with the rumour of apocalypse. The concepts of the Olivet sermon reflected the prophecies of Daniel, Joel and Isaiah, among others.

The theme of apocalypse was taken up by Paul; and, by John, was made the subject of the final book in the canon of Scripture. The suffering in the world is the greatest single indicator that the coming is close.

'One word of command, one shout from the archangel, one blast from the trumpet of God and the Lord himself will come down from Heaven! Those who have died in Christ will be the first to rise, and then we who are still living on the earth will be swept up with them in the clouds to meet the Lord in the air. And after that we shall be with him for ever.'[4]

'The day of the Lord will come as unexpectedly as a burglary to a householder. When men are saying "Peace and security" catastrophe will sweep down upon them as suddenly and inescapably as birth pangs to a pregnant woman.'[5]

' "As lightning flashes across from east to west so will the Son of Man's coming be. . . . the sun will be darkened, the moon will fail to give her light, the stars will fall from the sky, and the powers of heaven will be shaken. Then the sign of the Son of Man will appear in the sky, and all the nations of the earth will wring their hands as they see the Son of Man coming on the clouds of the sky in power and great splendour. And he will send out his angels with a loud trumpet-call and they will gather together his chosen from the four winds — from one end of the heavens to the other." ' [6]

' "Men's courage will fail completely as they realize what is threatening the world, for the very powers of heaven will be shaken. Then men will see the Son of Man coming in a cloud with great power and splendour! But when these things begin to happen, look up, hold your heads high, for you will soon be free." '[7]

The *purpose* of His coming is outlined in the apostles' creed; 'He shall come to judge the quick and the dead.' The Greek word 'to judge' means 'to distinguish', 'to separate', 'to sift'. The parables of Jesus explained the nature of divine judgement; the solemn process of sifting.

There will be rewards and punishments when He comes. The inevitability of the righteous judgement of God is fundamental to Scripture; it is set in train by the Second Advent. Vengeance, forbidden to us, will be a prerogative of God, exercised against the exploiters and the unjust. God's will be a just judgement.[8]

Jesus has unfinished business. At Calvary, evil and death were defeated. But in present imperfect, death still has dominion. It still takes faith, *strong* faith, to believe that evil will be beaten. But it will. At the Second Advent.

Above all, the Second Advent will bring deliverance. The idea of deliverance is strong in Scripture. Total deliverance will come on the day He comes.[9]

The first principle of God's government — freedom to choose — will obtain to the last; but, at the last, those who have taken the decision against good and God's government will take eternal consequences.[10]

The destroyer will be destroyed. Satan and his followers, death and the grave, stand before the judgement seat of God. They are condemned on their record, and destroyed by fire. It is the end of suffering, temptation, wickedness, pain and death. In the words of John Donne, 'And death shall be no more. Death, *thou* shalt die.'

History *is* shifting its gears. The pace *is* increasing. Man's hand is on the steering wheel. But the vehicle, though heading for a smash-up, is not totally out of control.

Behind all is the Hand of an all-powerful God who *will* intervene.

The Bible books of Daniel and the Revelation talk the language of apocalypse from start to finish. And to talk the language of apocalypse is to talk hope in a hopeless world. No hell conceived by human imagination could exceed in awfulness our own sick world in unending existence. Ecologists say things cannot go on. The Bible says things cannot go on. But the apocalypse of the scientist is a catastrophe that would send the entire human race into eternal oblivion. The apocalypse of the Bible is an *encounter* — with Jesus. An encounter that will leave our age truncated in Time, to make way for Eternity.

The problems of the world — all the hurting, the famine, the wars, the terrorism, the disease — are beyond solution. Politicians, scientists and medical researchers do not have the answers. The big screen industry is preoccupied with the supernatural and, though they are looking in the wrong direction, *the solution to the world's problems will be a supernatural one.* The only hope for the world is in an encounter with Jesus when He returns to the earth in splendour.

A huge shaft of dazzling light funnelling through the weeping blackness of what man has made of the world — swelling, expanding, dilating beyond the powers of pen to describe. And, in the midst, the One who has hurt with the hurting, comforted the sorrowing, returning to earth as a Conqueror, King of kings.

And, when His kingdom has been established . . . what?

' "He will wipe every tear from their eyes. There will be no more death or mourning or crying or pain, for the old order of things has passed away." He who was seated on the throne said, "I am making everything new!" ' [11]

' "The sun will no more be your light by day, nor will the brightness of the moon shine on you, for the Lord will be your everlasting light, and your God will be your glory . . . . Your days of sorrow will end." '[12]

' "Behold, I will create new heavens and a new earth. The former things will not be remembered, nor will they come to mind. . . . the sound of weeping and of crying will be heard . . . no more. Never again will there be . . . an infant who lives but a few days, ... The wolf and the lamb will feed together . . . . They will neither harm nor destroy in all my holy mountain," says the Lord.'[13]

Part of the old order that has passed away for ever will be every disease.

Marion will have no more bad days; her MS will be gone, her wheelchair redundant.

Alethea, who weeps for Andrew whose cancer, diagnosed only three months before, has killed him, will weep no more; Andrew will have been resurrected with a perfect body.

Sheila, whose heart aches for Mike — fighting, with the aid of chemo, his third bout with cancer — will walk with him into the painless morning of an eternal world.

Joy — 'Vivacious, Dedicated, Dearly Loved' — will take up the life so brutally cut short in that Christmas collision and live and love for ever.

Christopher Buckingham will laugh and play with Grandad again.

John and Edgar will not have to 'take it easy'; heart disease has been swept away with the old order and they can have life to the full.

AJ's blindness — and every other impediment of age — will have vanished, and he will be back to his studies.

The motor neuron disease that made Arthur's last year a hideous nightmare will have been forgotten and Iris will have him back in mint condition.

No miscarriage, cot death, accidents, arthritis, infirmity of any and every description; no famine, war, flood, earthquake or hurricane; no thorns in the flesh that inhibit life and diminish joy.

God *is* in the healing business and, when *all* are healed, the hurt will be removed from *His* life. And, instead of His being our source of strength in suffering, we shall know eternal joy in His company.

The 'eternal purpose', a 'purpose of the ages' — revealed in His Word, implemented through Jesus[14] — will have been accomplished. *Then* there will be peace on earth. God's government for ever vindicated.

Flashback to the Mount of the Ascension.

The Jesus known and loved by the disciples for three-and-a-half years had been removed from their sight. He had passed through time's hard shell, no longer to breathe earth's stale air, and had entered the eternal world to prepare a place for us.[15] The disciples gazed skyward. Suddenly two men dressed in white stood beside them; ' "Men of Galilee," they said, "why do you stand here looking into the sky? This same Jesus, who has been taken from you into heaven, will come back in the same way you have seen him go into heaven." '[16]

This same Jesus who confronted wild men and wilder seas and spoke calm to both; who touched the untouchable leper and lightened the blind beggar's darkness. *This same Jesus* whose word of forgiveness unlocked the rigid limbs of the paralytic and restored to self-respect the terrified girl caught in illicit passion. *This same Jesus* who blessed the babies and who turned to His mother in not-less-tender solicitude when His human frame was wracked by a crescendo of agony, whose lips spelt out the message, 'I place you in John's care'.[17] *This same loving, understanding*

Saviour who invites every troubled soul 'Come unto me, all ye that are weary and heavy laden, and I will give you rest.[18] *This same Jesus* the focus of healing and hope, now and for ever. *This same Jesus* will return, banish the old order for ever and, irreversibly, establish His eternal kingdom of health, peace and everlasting joy.

He concludes the canon of Scripture with the promise, ' "Yes, I am coming soon." ' Looking out over the pain-wretched world, who would not respond with John, 'Amen. Come, Lord Jesus'?[3]

---

[1] Revelation 22:2.

[2] Matthew 10:8; Luke 9:2.

[3] Matthew 24; Mark 13; Luke 21; John 14:1-3.

[4] 1 Thessalonians 4:16, 17, Phillips.

[5] 1 Thessalonians 5:2, 3, Phillips.

[6] Matthew 24:27, 29-31, Phillips.

[7] Luke 21:26-28, Phillips.

[8] 2 Thessalonians 1:7-10; Romans 12:19; 2 Thessalonians 1:8-10; Hebrews 9:28; Philippians 3:20, 21; Revelation 20-22.

[9] Daniel 12:1; John 14:3.

[10] 2 Thessalonians 2:8; Ephesians 3:10.

[11] Revelation 21:4, 5, NIV.

[12] Isaiah 60:19, 20, NIV.

[13] Isaiah 65:17-25, NIV.

[14] Ephesians 3:11; 1:9, 10.

[15] Acts 1:9; John 14:1-3.

[16] Acts 1:10, 11, NIV.

[17] See John 19:27.

[18] See Matthew 11:28.

[19] Revelation 22:20, NIV.